T0299188

DOING BUSINESS IN SOUTH ASIA

This concise textbook comprises selected case studies on the strategic challenges and opportunities faced by real-world organizations operating in South Asia.

The collection includes 15 short case studies from across the region, allowing easy comprehension and class discussion, and covers strategic management, localization strategies, strategic challenges, emerging global brands, digital transformation, sustainability, inclusive business, and economic development. Each case has corresponding reflective questions, references, and further reading and activities, making this a perfect comprehensive guide to help students understand and apply concepts to real-world situations.

Providing a solid understanding of the South Asian business environment, this is ideal recommended reading for advanced undergraduate and postgraduate students studying South Asian and International Business, Strategic Management, Emerging Markets, and Global Entrepreneurship.

Online, instructors will find complementary teaching notes to support learning.

G.V. Muralidhara is currently Director at ICFAI Business School Bengaluru, India. Prior to this, he was Dean at the renowned Case Research Center at ICFAI Business School Hyderabad, India. Muralidhara has authored or co-authored more than 150 case studies in management on a variety of topics.

His case *IKEA in Russia: Ethical Dilemmas* won the Ethics and Social Responsibility category at the Case Centre Awards and Competitions in 2016. He has also been successful at the EFMD case writing competition, winning the Latin American Business Cases category with *Chile's Concha y Toro: Successfully Selling 'New World' Wine Globally* in 2014, and the Emerging Chinese Global Competitors category with *Lenovo: Challenger to Leader* in 2013. Further awards include the Nominated award at the 2016 Global Contest for the 'Best China Focused Cases' for his case *Can Huawei Overcome Roadblocks in Its Quest for Global Markets?* and the first prize in the 2020 oikos Case Writing Competition for the case *Hello Tractor: Leveraging Technology to Provide Food Security & Sustainable Agriculture in Africa.*

He is currently Associate Editor for India-focused cases at the *International Journal of Instructional Cases.*

He has conducted many training programs on case method and case writing at various institutions.

International Cases in Business and Management

Series Editors: Gina Vega and Rob Edwards

This series of textbooks has been developed to provide students and lecturers with high-quality, peer-reviewed and concise teaching cases, which explore key business and management topics set in real-life scenarios around the world.

All cases included in each book are short – between 1500 and 2500 words – and are crafted to encourage class discussion and critical reflection. Cases are accompanied by a rich range of online resources for instructors, making effective and rewarding discussion in the classroom and corporate training room easy. All cases are real-world, with no composites and no invented situations. Some of them come from secondary sources, some from personal experience, and some from field research.

The series is suitable for all levels of university education, including MBA and Executive Education, and organizational training environments

Doing Business in South Asia
A Case Study Collection
Edited by G. V. Muralidhara

DOING BUSINESS IN SOUTH ASIA

A Case Study Collection

Edited by G.V. Muralidhara

LONDON AND NEW YORK

First published 2023
by Routledge
4 Park Square, Milton Park, Abingdon, Oxon OX14 4RN

and by Routledge
605 Third Avenue, New York, NY 10158

Routledge is an imprint of the Taylor & Francis Group, an informa business

British Library Cataloguing-in-Publication Data
A catalogue record for this book is available from the British Library

ISBN: 978-1-032-19851-4 (hbk)
ISBN: 978-1-032-19846-0 (pbk)
ISBN: 978-1-003-26115-5 (ebk)

DOI: 10.4324/9781003261155

Access the Support Material: www.routledge.com/9781032198460

Typeset in Bembo
by Apex CoVantage, LLC

CONTENTS

ACKNOWLEDGEMENTS

The motivation for this volume came from Dr. Gina Vega, who initiated this interesting project along with Routledge. My association with her started with a case study on disaster management that I co-authored for the PMI Teaching Case competition. Gina was the reviewer for the case and she provided very good inputs to refine our submission. The case won the PMI Teaching Case Award in 2016. Then, I started reviewing cases for the International Journal of Instructional Cases and subsequently became the Associate Editor for India focused cases. I am extremely grateful to her and Rob Edwards for reposing confidence in me to edit the first volume in the series and supporting throughout this project with useful inputs.

The most difficult part of editing a case volume is getting good contributions from authors. I have tried obtaining contributions from authors across South Asia. I am thankful to all the contributing authors for their perseverance in going through several rounds of reviews.

I would not have been able to complete this volume without the assistance of Indu Parepu in reviewing the cases. I thank her for her involvement and contribution throughout the project.

My institution has always provided motivation and encouragement to faculty members to undertake such endeavours. I am grateful to the management for the same.

Sophia Levine, Senior Editor, Marketing & Strategy Textbooks at Routledge has been extremely supportive and understanding in responding promptly and guiding me along in this project. I thank her for her support and hope that I will be able to work with her in many more projects in future. I am grateful to Rupert Spurrier, Editorial Assistant for his assistance in taking this volume to production.

Taking up this project meant sacrificing many holidays and weekends as well as investing all my spare time on this work. My family has supported me and provided me the space required to complete it successfully.

Finally, my thanks are due to Routledge for taking up publication of this volume and the series.

FIGURES

TABLES

CONTRIBUTORS

Afsana Akhtar Assistant Professor, BRAC Business School, BRAC University, Dhaka, Bangladesh

R. Bala Subramanian Assistant Professor, RAJAGIRI Business School, RAJAGIRI College of Social Sciences, Kochi, India

D.B. Bharati Director, Rajgad Institute of Management Research and Development, Pune, India

Kohinoor Biswas Assistant Professor, Department of Business Administration, East West University, Dhaka, Bangladesh

Rupali Chaudhuri Pursuing Ph.D. in HR and OB at the ICFAI Foundation for Higher Education, a Deemed-to-be University, under Section 3 of the UGC Act, 1956, Hyderabad, India. Research interests include diversity management and HR analytics.

Segufta Dilshad Senior Lecturer, Department of Public Health, North South University, Dhaka, Bangladesh

Kranti K. Dugar Assistant Professor of Marketing at the University of Wisconsin – Eau Claire's College of Business. His teaching interests include new product development, consumer behaviour, global marketing, marketing strategy, marketing research, and international immersion programmes. Most recently, he has been teaching in the University of Wisconsin MBA Consortium, which was ranked #9 among 358 online programmes in the country by the US News & World Report.

Sanjay Fuloria Professor of Operations and IT at ICFAI Business School, Hyderabad; Director at the Centre for Distance and Online Education; and Coordinator, Centre of Excellence for Digital Transformation at the ICFAI Foundation for Higher Education, a Deemed-to-be University, under Section 3 of the UGC Act, 1956, Hyderabad, India

K.B.S. Kumar Assistant Professor, Department of Human Resources, ICFAI Business School, Hyderabad, India; author of five books in the areas of leadership, entrepreneurship and emotional intelligence. He is Consulting Editor of the magazine *Effective Executive*; author of teaching case studies in the areas of leadership, strategy, and entrepreneurship.

N. Manjula Associate Professor (Marketing Area), Thiagarajar School of Management, Madurai, India

Ujjal Mukherjee Associate Professor and Area Head, Organization Behaviour and Human Resource Management, Faculty of Management Studies, CMS Business School, Jain (Deemed-to-be-University), Bengaluru, India

G.V. Muralidhara Professor and Director, ICFAI Business School, Bangalore, India, a constituent of the ICFAI Foundation for Higher Education, a Deemed-to-be University under Section 3 of the UGC Act, 1956, Hyderabad, India

Bhagyashree Narayan Research Scholar in Financial Management at Savitribai Phule Pune University and Visiting Faculty at NMIMS, a Deemed-to-be University, Navi Mumbai, India

Harold Andrew Patrick Professor and Dean, Organization Behaviour and Human Resource Management, Faculty of Management Studies, CMS Business School, Jain (Deemed-to-be-University), Bengaluru, India

S.S.M. Sadrul Huda Associate Professor, Department of Management, SBE, North South University, Dhaka, Bangladesh

Mohammad Salman Assistant Professor, Organization Behaviour and Human Resource Management, Faculty of Management Studies, CMS Business School, Jain (Deemed-to-be-University), Bengaluru, India

M. Sayeed Alam Assistant Professor, Department of Business Administration, East West University, Dhaka, Bangladesh

M.H. Sharieff Professor of Practice, Marketing, Faculty of Management Studies, CMS Business School, Jain (Deemed-to-be-University), Bengaluru, India

Md. Ishtiake Uddin Associate Professor, European University of Bangladesh and Doctoral Student, Faculty of Business and Economics, University of Malaya, Malaysia

K.S. Venu Gopal Rao Professor and Area Head, Marketing & Strategy at the ICFAI Business School, Hyderabad, a constituent of the ICFAI Foundation for Higher Education, a Deemed-to-be University, under Section 3 of the UGC Act, 1956, Hyderabad, India

INTRODUCTION

This volume featuring selected case studies on events, situations, issues, leadership, and organizations relating to South Asia is part of the casebook series – International Cases in Business and Management being brought out by Taylor and Francis.

Asia is expected to contribute 50% of the global GDP by 2040 and drive 40% of the world's consumption. This represents a real shift in the world's centre of gravity. South Asia comprising Bangladesh, Bhutan, India, Pakistan, Nepal, Sri Lanka, Afghanistan, and Maldives constitutes an important part of this development.

There is increasing interest among institutions and organizations across the world to learn more about Asia. Major case repositories have been increasingly featuring cases related to this region. Case studies related to Asia form an essential component of the course curriculum in many leading institutions.

In 2016, writing in his book *The Rise and Fall of Nations*, Ruchir Sharma highlighted the quiet growth of South Asian countries. He pointed out that the nations of South Asia were growing at a healthy average annual growth rate of 6%. Apart from progressive economic reforms in the countries and healthy credit growth, he pointed out the strong growth in working-age population as a positive factor for the steady growth of the countries in South Asia.

The year 2022 presented a slightly different picture than what was projected earlier. Like other countries across the globe, South Asian nations were also impacted by the COVID-19 pandemic that caused severe hardships to economies and societies. Post the pandemic, the Russia–Ukraine conflict brought in newer problems for these countries.

In 2022, India was making efforts to recover from the effects of the pandemic and also control inflation in the economy. Hit by the loss of revenue from tourism and disruption in economic activities, Sri Lanka was going through the worst economic crisis in its post-independence history. Similarly, Pakistan was going through serious economic challenges amidst internal turbulence. Though Bangladesh weathered the pandemic successfully, the residual impact of the changes was being felt by the country. In addition to the impact of these changes, being an island country, Maldives was also facing the challenges due to global warming and rising sea levels. Afghanistan was trying to find its feet, after a regime change, amidst global sanctions.

DOI: 10.4324/9781003261155-1

The world was keenly watching how the South Asian nations would navigate the challenges and march ahead during the next few decades.

This volume will definitely provide important resources to instructors who want to use contemporary case studies on South Asia in their curriculum and to students who want to understand this region better.

PART I

Introductory Chapter

Success in a Case Class – Resource for Students

1

CASE PREPARATION AND ANALYSIS FOR STUDENTS[1]

Gina Vega and Rob Edwards

It is not that I'm so smart. But I stay with the questions much longer.

–Albert Einstein

Why Are You in This Class?

Perhaps you are focusing your studies on challenges specific to South Asia. Perhaps you are taking this class as an elective. Maybe you are a business major who wants to learn a bit more about the issues that companies in Bangladesh, Bhutan, India, Pakistan, Nepal, Afghanistan, and Maldives are facing. Maybe this class was the only one open that fit into your schedule.

None of these matters. What does matter is your willingness to participate in your own learning, rather than wait for someone to *tell* you what to learn.

What to Expect from a Case-based Class

If you are used to a traditional lecture format class, a case class will be a big change for you.

In a traditional class, you are the recipient of knowledge. The instructor is the giver of knowledge, and you receive her words of wisdom passively.

In a case class, you are the creator of knowledge and the discoverer of insights. The instructor is your guide and your facilitator, and she shares in the creation and discovery processes with you.

In a traditional class, the instructor works hard, and you sit quietly. You can send in a tape recorder and listen to the lecture later. You can watch a video and play computer games. You can check your email. You can update your Facebook account.

In a case class, you both work hard and are very much present. You are alert the whole time, because you are responsible for your learning and the learning processes of your classmates. Case learning is social learning and requires active involvement.

DOI: 10.4324/9781003261155-3

Here's how it works:

- You read the assigned case ahead of class. You might consider trying the Three Reads Model in Appendix 1.1.
    - Take notes as to the individuals involved, the situations presented, and any connections you can make to theory or analogous characters or situations you have been exposed to before, either in classes or in your work or life experience.
    - Identify your assumptions and the information that is missing for you to do a thorough analysis.
    - List the problems and select one problem to focus on at a time. Most cases present multiple problems; your ability to identify a key problem will give your case analysis structure and meaning.
    - Do any preliminary analysis you can, such as financial comparisons and ratios, statistical analyses, or other quantitative explorations. If your analysis is to be qualitative, determine the foundation of your analysis and articulate reasons for and against a strategy or position.
    - Write down as many possible recommendations as you can, then select one and commit to it.
- Go to class and get ready for an engaged discussion.
    - The instructor may start off with a précis of the case (or ask you to provide one) and then toss out some icebreaker questions – easy questions to get the conversation moving.
    - The instructor may continue to toss questions to the group or, depending on personal style, may ask questions or opinions directly of one individual.
    - The instructor will tease out a series of analyses, decision-making perspectives, and positions from the class members.
    - The class reaches a conclusion, recommendation, decision, or final analysis.
- You may be assigned to a team.
    - If you have been assigned to a case team before the classroom discussion, your preparation should take place with this team.
    - You can expect a lot of lively discussion during the preparation phase, and you will generally (but not always) come to agreement before class.
    - The class discussion will be between team positions rather than individual positions and will proceed as mentioned earlier.

Hints for Success in a Case Class

- Be prepared
- Participate actively
- Allow your emotions to become involved along with your critical analysis
- Respect your peers' input
- Try to understand the alternative perspectives put forth in the classroom
- If on a team, be a 'good' team member – no one likes a free rider

Two Different Types of Cases

There are two different kinds of cases: decision-based cases and descriptive or illustrative cases.

In either kind of case, your job will be clear to you, if not from the narrative, then from the questions that follow the case. Be sure to read and think about those questions and use them as guidance in your analysis.

Preparing a Written Case Analysis

The cases in this book are short, designed specifically to help you focus on the key aspects of problems presented. You will, of course, find information in the cases that is not directly relevant to the main problem. Pay attention to this information, as it is likely to be important in your analysis. However, it will not drive your analysis, which should be focused, instead, on the topical components presented in each case.

The analysis of a full-length case can be expected to take a significant amount of time to complete. The analysis of a short case should be, by its nature, short. It will contain all (or most) of the elements described later in the text, but the elements will be short and concise. It is likely that your analysis will include answers to (or take direction from) the questions at the end of the case.

TABLE 1.1 Types of Cases

Decision-based Cases		*Descriptive or Illustrative Cases*
Description	Decision-based cases will require you to make a reasoned recommendation, supported by facts and theory, for the case protagonist to follow	Descriptive or illustrative cases do not conclude with a call for a recommendation. Instead, they present a situation that has occurred and your job is to analyse the protagonist's actions
Example	Your recommendation might be for the protagonist to seek alternative sources of funding rather than depending on friends and family. Some sources he might consider include a bank line of credit, loans, or angel investors. These three sources involve less emotional investment and more straightforward financial analysis to convince lenders	You may determine that she should have taken a different set of action steps that might have led to a better outcome. Or you may decide that the actions taken were justified and provided the best outcomes under the existing circumstances. Or, your recommendation might be to take advantage of a favourable economy to expand now rather than waiting until the company has accumulated more assets. Even though the protagonist tends to be conservative in his approach to expansion, it makes sense to exploit opportunities that present themselves. It may be a less secure position to take, but the potential rewards may be greater

Although it may sound easy to write a short case analysis, do not allow yourself to be tricked into thinking that such an analysis is a snap to put together. It requires discipline to write concisely and to explain complex concepts using simple, clear language. That will be your challenge throughout this course. The examples included in this chapter are based on finance; your cases will likely have a different focus.

Written Analysis of a Short Decision-based Finance Case

If you are preparing for a class discussion, the Three Reads Method (Appendix 1.1) will suffice. However, if you have been assigned a *written analysis of a decision-based* case, it can be hard to know where to start. The following model can help you complete a clear and organized decision-based analysis. You can generally use tables, formulas, or matrices instead of narrative sentences if they will support your analysis better.

1. *Executive Summary*
   Write this section last even though it appears first in the case analysis. The goal of the executive summary is to provide a *brief* overview of the main issues, the proposed recommendation, and the actions to follow. (two or three sentences)
2. *Statement of the Problem*
   Describe the core problem(s) of the case and the decision(s) to be made by the protagonist. Include the symptoms of the problem(s) and differentiate them from the problem(s) themselves. For example, the spots on your face are a symptom. The problem is that you have the measles (or acne, or an allergy to some skin product, or some other infection). This statement of the problem is a *diagnostic process*, and you need to build the rationale for your diagnosis into this section. (two or three sentences)
3. *Causes*
   This section is an exploration and discussion of potential causes of the main case problem(s). Support your exploration by the application of relevant theories from this course or others. Be sure to use analytical tools that will support your decision-making process and will illustrate your analysis. (two or three sentences)
4. *Possible Solutions/Alternatives*
   Surface as many possible solutions or alternative actions as you can. You should not limit your possibilities to what you think is easy to accomplish or logical, but rather entertain a wide variety of options. You do not have to recommend all of these options, but you need to make your instructor aware that you have considered them. (two or three sentences)
5. *Selection of Criteria and Analysis of Alternatives*
   Select the criteria for determining the basic feasibility of the alternatives identified earlier. These criteria will guide you in considering the pros and cons of each feasible alternative. Consider at least three alternatives in this section. Sometimes, a tabular format will keep this section organized and clear. You should be prepared to provide financial analyses in this section. (two or three sentences or small matrix)
6. *Recommendation*
   What do you recommend that the protagonist do? Support your recommendation with a rationale that is based both in facts and in the appropriate theory for the problem

(i.e. market analysis, financial statements analysis, the impact of organizational structure, supply chain management, or other disciplinary focus). (two or three sentences)

7. *Implementation*

   Your instructor may state that no case analysis is complete without providing the action steps to implement the recommendation. What steps should the protagonist take in order to make your recommendation happen? Identify to the greatest extent possible the responsibilities, costs, timeline, and measurement of success of the final implementation.

Appendix 1.2 provides a sample written analysis of a short decision case.

Written Analysis of a Short Descriptive or Illustrative Finance Case

If you are preparing for a class discussion, the method mentioned earlier or the Three Reads Method at the end of the chapter will suffice. However, if you have been assigned a *written analysis of a descriptive or illustrative finance case*, it can be hard to know where to start. The following model can help you complete a clear and organized analysis. You can generally use tables, formulas, or matrices instead of narrative sentences if they will support your analysis better.

1. *Executive Summary*

   Write this section last even though it appears first in the case analysis. The goal of the executive summary is to provide a *brief* overview of the main issues, your analysis, and your conclusions. (two or three sentences)

2. *The Facts*

   This is not simply a list of case facts. You need to determine which facts are relevant and which are simply background information or environmental 'noise.' If you are analysing a business ethics case, for example, it probably does not matter that the action takes place in the fall. However, in a finance case it may well matter that the action occurs at the end of a sales period, a fiscal year, or at some other critical period.

   Draw facts not only from the case narrative but, notably, from the exhibits, attachments, financial records, spreadsheets, and other sources within the case. Be sure to peruse these figures carefully for possible errors, misinterpretations, and potential clues to case solutions. (bulleted list)

3. *Inferences to Be Drawn*

   Why did things happen as they did? What else might happen as a consequence? What are the implications of these actions in terms of attitudes and relationships? Financial decisions, especially in entrepreneurial environments, are rarely based solely on the numbers. Numbers are generally rational, while people rarely are, and their decisions reflect this. (two or three sentences)

4. *Theory- and Technique-based Discussion of the Case Action*

   Apply relevant theory and financial analysis techniques to an explanation of actions and consequences, implications of actions and consequences, and the impact of various outcome criteria on the decisions that were made in the case. The true value of learning entrepreneurial finance lies in the use of actual data to guide future decisions and to draw sensible conclusions about potential outcomes. The financial analyses help you look to the future as well as reflect on the past. (two or three sentences)

5. *Options to the Actions within the Case*
   Compare the actions of the protagonist with the other courses of action that were open at the time. What might have been the logical outcomes of those actions? Determine a hierarchy of preferred actions based on outcome criteria you established in part 4. This section may logically take a tabular format.
6. *Conclusion/Reflection*
   This is your rationale for preferred action. If the protagonist has done the right thing according to your analysis, explain why. If the protagonist should have done something else, explain why. Reflect on your reasoning. In a descriptive or illustrative case, your reflection is often the most valuable section because it is from these reflections that future courses of action will derive. (two or three sentences)

Appendix 1.3 provides a sample written analysis of a short descriptive case.

How Will Your Written Case Analysis Be Evaluated?

Because case evaluation can be highly subjective, many instructors will prepare a rubric for you to measure your own work against. You can find a basic rubric that outlines generic instructor's expectations and clarifies the standard you should be aiming for in Appendix 1.4. Each instructor's rubric is unique, but the generic rubric provides some guidelines for you to follow.

Appendix 1.5 is a self-grading rubric to help you check your own work for completeness before submission. This self-grader will help to keep you 'honest.'

APPENDIX 1.1

Preparing for a Case Discussion: The Three Reads Model for a Short Case

Reading and preparing a case for class discussion involves more than reading a blog, your email, a novel, or a chapter in a textbook. You can develop your case reading skills through the technique outlined next. This technique allows you to make the best possible contribution during the class case discussion. It requires you to read the case (even short cases) three times, twice briefly and once extensively. If you are working with a team, you will want to adapt this process to assure topical coverage.

First Read

- Find 6 minutes (yes, 6 minutes is enough for the one-to-four-page cases in this book) to sit down uninterrupted. Mute your phone so that you do not get distracted during this short reading period.
- Read the book. This may be several paragraphs long in a full-length case, but just one or two sentences in the cases in this book. The book will introduce you to the case 'problem.' Jot down the problem in the margin.
- Read the first sentence (and only the first sentence) of each paragraph in the case. Write a keyword or two in the margin next to the paragraph.
- Read the titles only of any attachments and exhibits.
- Turn your phone back on and go about your business.

Second Read

- This is the big one – a two-page case will take you at least 30 minutes. Remember that if you have interruptions, this period must be extended.
- Read the entire case, slowly and carefully. Jot notes as you go along about the characters and their behaviour, the situation and the action. Sometimes preparing a timeline of action makes it easier to follow and remember. Be sure to include any exhibits and attachments during this read.
- Jot down your own response to the situation and the characters, even if it's unsupported by theories or formal concepts. Make any connections you can to analogous situations

you have experienced or read about. What are the differences or similarities to this situation? Remember, these notes that you are making are yours alone – no one else will be looking at them. It doesn't matter if they are messy, have lines drawn all over them, are put together in right-brain or left-brain style, just as long as they exist. They are meant to help you.

- Make a list of the assumptions you are making, the financial analyses you need to conduct, and the information you still need before you make a recommendation. Something is always missing, or the case would be really boring. So, what is missing?
- List the alternative solutions to the case, their pros and cons, and then select one recommendation. You always have to commit to one recommendation and provide a rationale for it. This recommendation should be supported by theory, experience, quantitative analysis, or other rationale.
- Prepare any case questions you have been assigned. Be sure to check any spreadsheets for errors or misinterpretations.
- You should be tired at this point. Put the case away.

Third Read

- This last read takes place not too long before class. The point of it is to make sure that the case is fresh in your mind and that you are still comfortable with your recommendation.
- This read resembles the first read: read the beginning, the first sentence of each paragraph, and so on. But this time include both your marginal notes and the notes you have made during the second read. You will need these notes to participate actively in class. Remember that class participation means that you have to talk – it's OK to read aloud what you have written if you are uncomfortable talking off the cuff.
- The entire process has taken 2 hours or less, which is about two-thirds the amount of time you should anticipate using for class preparation for a 1½ hour class. If your class period is longer than this, your preparation should be commensurately more extensive.

APPENDIX 1.2

Sample Written Case Analysis for a Short Decision-based Finance Case[2]

Executive Summary

Koehler Propane was a small, family-owned propane dealer with a very small heating oil division inherited through a prior acquisition. A local heating oil dealer was put up for sale and Koehler had to decide whether or not to purchase it, and if so, at what price and on what terms. The best strategy for Koehler is to offer a cash price of between $800 and $850,000.

Statement of the Problem

The propane and heating oil dealer industry was in the declining phase of its life cycle and was characterized by high fluctuations in revenue due to uncertainty in energy prices and weather, high fixed assets requirement, and regulations by both federal and state agencies. Competition was high and business growth either involved intense price competition or acquisition of competing companies. Koehler and his son had to decide whether to buy the heating oil company or to close down their own small heating oil division altogether.

Causes

Some of Koehler's current equipment needed replacement if he were to remain in the heating oil business. Koehler had an advantage over competing bidders in a cash deal but not in a stock deal. The four valuation methods (discounted cash flow valuation and multiples valuation, multiples valuation, EBITDA multiple method, and percent of annual sales + inventory method) range from $624,019 to $918,606, averaging $818,469. A reasonable cash price ranged from $800,000 to $850,000

Possible Solutions/Alternatives

Koehler Propane had three alternatives:

- *Close down the oil business:* Closing down the heating oil business would eliminate a break-even/money-losing division and allow Koehler to stay focused on its core business

TABLE 1.2 Selection of Criteria and Analysis of Alternatives

Criterion	*Assigned Value*	*Pros*	*Cons*
Growth	40	They want to be industry leaders, larger customer base	Declining industry, high competition
Diversification	30	One of the main business goals	High risk, expensive
Capital investment	30	More dependable equipment	Potential dedication of needed cash to non-liquid assets

of propane delivery but it would be contrary to their vision of developing Koehler into a large energy company.

- *Purchase two new trucks to replace existing ones:* Purchasing new trucks required capital investments into a potentially money losing division. Given the low volume and the surcharge they had to pay due to lack of bulk storage, they were at a cost disadvantage, severely limiting their ability to compete on price.
- *Acquire the heating oil company:* This would advance Koehler towards a more diverse product line and increase the size of its business. It would provide Koehler bulk storage facilities and make them a major heating oil distributor in the vicinity. If Koehler failed to acquire the heating oil company, one of its competitors would gain entrance into its primary territory and Koehler would face increased competition in its propane business.

Selection of Criteria and Analysis of Alternatives

Note that the assignment of values for the three alternatives is arbitrary and meant as an example only. You would assign values as relevant for your own analysis.

Recommendation

Closing down the oil business is bad for growth, for diversification, and for capital investment. If quantified, the option has zero value. Purchasing two new trucks is good for capital investment, but 'iffy' for both growth and diversification. If quantified, the option has a potential value of 30+. Acquiring the heating oil company is good for growth, diversification, and capital investment. Quantified, the option has a potential value of 100.

Both companies are located in the same town, and the two owners have past business relationships; therefore, Koehler will have better knowledge of the oil company than competing bidders. Competing bidders may be unwilling to offer a cash deal, or they will likely offer a much lower cash price. Koehler has an advantage over competing bidders in a cash deal but not in a stock deal. Given the advantages of a cash deal to the oil company, the best strategy for Koehler is to offer a cash price.

Implementation

1. Agree on a valuation
2. Structure the deal internally
3. Negotiate with the seller for a mutually agreeable acquisition

APPENDIX 1.3

Sample Written Case Analysis for a Short Descriptive/Illustrative Finance Case[3]

1. **Executive Summary**
   A schoolteacher has decided to open a taqueria in a small, historic New England city. The problem is whether he should launch his business at the time of the case in light of the many challenges facing him. He could not provide all the necessary information and was reluctant to listen to advice. He should not launch his business at this time.
2. **The Facts**
   The entrepreneur knew a little bit about a lot of things, but not enough about any one of the functional elements of his business to run it on his own. He had insufficient funds to last through a dry spell; he was being pushed to launch because the landlord of his desired location was in a hurry to get the lease signed. He did not have a full liquor license. Money was tight, loans were non-existent, and his debt to asset ratio did not approach the industry standard. It also looks like he needs to do a closer examination of his anticipated revenues.
3. **Inferences to be Drawn**
   The Howling Wolf is likely to create value for the customer, as there appears to be growing demand for this type of cuisine and there is little direct competition. However, the money-making potential of the restaurant is unclear, and the owner's ability to sustain operations with the proposed family/friends staff is doubtful. A launch would be a high risk/minimal reward strategy.
4. **Theory- and Technique-based Discussion of the Case Action**
   A SWOT analysis showed that he had some significant strengths and opportunities in terms of personal contacts and an opening in the restaurant market. His passion, product and service differentiation, and personal skills suggest that he can provide an appealing venue for locals to enjoy a unique culinary experience. Potential funders have not been found, the economy is weak (although beginning to rebound slightly), and money is scarce. Although the entrepreneur believes strongly in his restaurant, he has been unable to provide financials that support that belief for banks or other funders. Computing breakeven revenue and cash burn rate show that breakeven weekly revenue is 4.35% below the original estimate. Total monthly cash outflow excluding COGS is over

$34,000 compared to a beginning cash balance of only $61,000. If revenue is more than 23% below the original estimate, he will run out of cash in six months.

5. **Options to the Actions within the Case**
Decision criteria: Potential to make a good return. Likelihood of staying in business without a liquor license. Potential to survive on limited investment. Likelihood of family and friends to continue providing low-cost assistance.
The entrepreneur has to weight the importance of each of the decision criteria before making his decision. There are two possible decisions that the entrepreneur could take:
    - The entrepreneur could open based on the support that he had from his family and his experience with this type of cuisine and confidence that the tourist season would likely be able to cover the slow season.
    - The entrepreneur could postpone opening until acquiring more funds, a liquor license, and business advisors.

6. **Conclusion/Reflection**
Based on the aforementioned analyses, I would not recommend launching the business at this time. I think the entrepreneur should find an angel or other investor to provide the financial stability that will cover him through the tough times during the first year of operations. He should continue his efforts to obtain a full liquor license. He should plan to invest in advertising prior to his launch, and he should conduct a full-scale location analysis prior to signing his lease.

APPENDIX 1.4

Generic Grading Rubric

How Will My Written Case Analysis Be Evaluated?

Because evaluation can be highly subjective, many instructors will prepare a rubric for you to measure your own work against. This rubric outlines the instructor's expectations and clarifies the standard you should be aiming for. Each instructor's rubric is unique, but the generic rubric that follows provides some guidelines for you to follow.

TABLE 1.3 Case Analysis Evaluation

Suggested Criteria	*Poor, Weak, Needs Improvement*	*Satisfactory, Acceptable, Good*	*Outstanding, Exemplary, Excellent*
Thoroughness	One or more required section is missing or treated perfunctorily X points	All required sections are addressed to a great extent X points	All required sections are addressed completely X points
Theoretical relevance	The analysis does not incorporate relevant theories X points	Addresses theories and course concepts appropriately X points	Addresses theories and concepts appropriately and insightfully X points
Quality of analysis	Does not suggest careful thought or provide insights X points	Analysis suggests both effort and understanding of the material X points	Detailed analysis that offers careful and logical inferences X points
Conclusions or implementation	Unsupported or missing arguments overlook salient issues X points	Supported arguments capture main issues X points	Supported arguments address both main issues and subtle or secondary problems X points
Writing quality	Careless writing, many grammar and spelling errors, poor organization X points	Clear writing, few grammar and spelling errors, organized presentation X points	Flawless writing, clear organization, correct grammar and spelling X points

APPENDIX 1.5

Self-grading Rubric

Use This Rubric to Evaluate the Quality of Your Own Work before You Hand It In

TABLE 1.4 Self-grading Rubric

	Something Is Wrong	*Everything Is Correct*	*Student Comment Here*
Presence of all required elements (refer to original assignment)	What is missing? Add it	In the column to the right, list the items that appear in the Table of Contents	
Issues	Some primary or secondary issues are missing	All the primary and secondary issues have been dealt with and prioritized	
Adequacy of discussion of consequences, depth of data analysis, application of theory	Weak in one or more of the listed areas	Issues are fully developed, including alternatives, consequences clearly spelled out, data analysis is comprehensive, and theory is applied correctly	
Quality of expression	I have not run Spellcheck or Grammarcheck. I have not had someone else proofread my work	My work has been proofread by someone else and all errors have been corrected	
Would I be willing to turn in this report to my employer?	If no – fix it!	If yes, you're done. Hand it in	
What grade would you give this project?	C or less	A or B	

Notes

1 Adapted from *Entrepreneurial Finance: Concepts and Cases, Second Edition* by Miranda S Lam and Gina Vega, Copyright (2021) by Routledge Taylor & Francis. Reproduced by permission of Taylor & Francis Group.
2 This abbreviated analysis was prepared from *The Offer Price* (M Lam and R Luther, 2012, The CASE Journal, Vol 8.2).
3 This abbreviated analysis was prepared from the *Howling Wolf Taqueria: Feeding the Good Wolf* (G Vega and M Lam, 2013, Case Research Journal, Vol 34, Issue 2).

PART II
Strategic Management

2

AIR INDIA

Can Tata Group Bring Back the Glory and Make It Profitable Too?

G.V. Muralidhara

Synopsis

The case study discusses the acquisition of Air India, the national flag carrier of India, by the Tata Group, a prominent business group in India. The privatization of Air India and selecting the Tata Group as the successful bidder marked a full circle for Air India as it had originally been started by the Tata Group in 1932 and had been subsequently nationalized by the government in 1953. Air India was once known for its distinctive and excellent service. But, over the years the performance of the airline had deteriorated and it had accumulated huge losses, in the aftermath of which the government of India decided to privatize the airline. Though it was a momentous occasion for the Tata Group, the task of turning around the loss-making Air India and making it profitable looked quite daunting. There was a need to improve the operational efficiency and cut costs, in addition to bringing customer-oriented and result-oriented culture. The challenge was compounded by the fact that the Indian aviation market was highly competitive and had witnessed the exit of many players due to continued losses. In addition, both Vistara and Air Asia India, in which the Tata Group had major stakes, were making losses as at 2021. The Tata Group had a major task of turning around the loss-making airline and reinstating its past glory.

Introduction

On October 8, 2021, the Government of India declared Tata Sons, the holding company of the Tata Group as the winning bidder of the government-owned airline, Air India, the national flag carrier. By doing so, the government was giving the airline with accumulated losses of Rs.840 billion[1] (as at 2020) back to its founder, after nationalizing it in 1953.[2]

Air India, previously known as Tata Aviation Service, was started by JRD Tata (JRD),[3] a passionate aviator in 1932. The name was changed to Tata Airlines in 1938. JRD Tata had built Tata Airlines into an efficient air service operator with a 33% market share in the

DOI: 10.4324/9781003261155-5

country by 1946.[4] It was renamed to Air India after it became a public company in 1946. In 1948, it operated the first international flight as Air India International. In 1953, the government nationalized all the private airlines and formed Air India and Indian Airlines for international and domestic operations, respectively.

In 2007, Air India and Indian Airlines were merged to form a single entity, Air India.[5]

Though Air India was associated with India, it carried a rich legacy and had a substantial number of slots at major airports in India and across the world. But it had lost market share to private airlines over the years.[6] In 2020, Air India and Air India Express had a combined market share of 19.3% of international traffic in the country and 11% in the domestic market[7] (see Table 2.1).

Tata eventually ventured back into aviation business by starting its own airline Vistara, and also partnered with Malaysia-based Air Asia to start Air Asia India. Though the Tata Group had a strong brand name in India and globally, its airline businesses Air Asia India and Vistara were loss-making entities as at 2021.

Air India came back into the fold of Tata Group in 2021, 68 years after it had been taken over by the government. With the acquisition of Air India, the Tata Group got a company that was debt ridden, over staffed, had a low staff morale, inefficient, and was losing market share to better-run competitors. At the same time the industry has been one of those that has been adversely impacted due to COVID-19.

Considering the numerous challenges the Tata Group would have to tackle issues, namely, improving operational efficiency, cost cutting, and improving the work culture, it was a question mark if Tatas would be able to successfully bring back the glory and make Air India profitable in the near future.[8] It remained to seen how Tatas would make Air India fly high again.

Growth of Tata Group

Beginning with a textile mill in 1877, the Tata Group steadily expanded to a number of different industries and businesses, including steel, hotels, engineering, oil, chemicals, power, tea, and information technology. JRD led the group from 1938 to 1991 and established the group as a prominent business group in India with a focus on ethics, governance, and employee welfare. Under JRD's leadership, Tata Group's turnover increased from Rs.170 million in 1939

TABLE 2.1 Air India: Fleet Size and Routes Operated

Fleet Size (in 2021)

	Air India	*Air India Express*
Owned	70	17
Leased	58	8
Total	128	25

Routes Operated

Air India operated 444 international routes during winter 2019 and 427 international routes in summer 2019. It operated 342 domestic routes in 2021.

Source: airindia.in/fleet-details.htm; airindia.in/annualreport-2019–2020.htm; airindia.in/time-table.htm

to Rs.100,000 million in 1991. The number of companies in the group grew from 14 to 95.[9] During his 50 years of leadership of the group, JRD had led the group through personal example and established it as a group that was both value- and market-driven. From 1991 to 2012, the group was led by Ratan Tata.[10] His stint was marked by consolidation of the group and global expansion. Under his leadership the group's revenues grew to a size of Rs.4,757 billion by 2012, more than half of which was contributed by international operations[11] (see Table 2.2).

Air India: The Beginning

JRD was born in the pioneering industrial family of the Tatas. Jamshedji Tata, the founder of the group, established Tata Sons in 1887. He was not only a pioneering and progressive industrialist but also a philanthropist who believed in the advancement of India. Born to a

TABLE 2.2 List of Companies in the Tata Group*

Vertical	*Companies*
Technology	Tata Consultancy Services
	Tata Elxsi
	Tata Digital
Steel	Tata Steel
Auto	Tata Motors
	Jaguar Land Rover
	Tata Autocomp Systems
Consumer and Retail	Tata Chemicals
	Tata Consumer Products
	Titan Company
	Voltas
	Infiniti Retail
	Trent
Infrastructure	Tata Power
	Tata Projects
	Tata Consulting Engineers
	Tata Realty and Infrastructure
	Tata Housing
Financial Services	Tata Capital
	Tata AIA Life
	Tata AIG
	Tata Asset Management Company
Aerospace and Defence	Tata Advanced Systems
Tourism and Travel	Indian Hotels
	Tata SIA Airlines
	Air Asia (India)
Telecom and Media	Tata Communications
	Tata Play
	Tata Teleservices
Trading and Investment	Tata International
	Tata Industries
	Tata Investment Corporation

* Prior to acquisition of Air India.

Source: tata.com/investors/companies

French mother, JRD spent much of his childhood in France. His fascination for aviation started right from childhood, being in a neighbourhood where Louis Bleriot, an aviation enthusiast, lived, in a place called Hardelot. JRD obtained his flying licence in 1929, when he was 25 years old. Adventurous by nature, in 1930, JRD took up the 'Prize for England–India Flight' challenge which invited persons of Indian nationality to complete a solo flight between England and India within six weeks. Sensing an opportunity for air transportation, in 1932, JRD started Tata Aviation Service which transported mail between Karachi and Bombay.[12] The company established a reputation for reliability and punctuality. The coverage was later expanded to other locations and to carry passengers as well. Starting with just two aircrafts, within five years the fleet had expanded to 15 planes. By 1946, Tata Airlines was carrying every third air passenger in the country. In the same year, it became a public company and was renamed Air India. In 1948, Air India, along with participation from the government of India and the public, started Air India International to offer international flights.

A Culture of Excellence: Creating a World Class Airline

JRD had a clear vision of the future of air travel as early as 1943 when he envisioned that air travel would become popular in 20 or 30 years just like trains or steamers. He believed that Air India would be successful only if it could offer something unique to the air travellers. As the Chairman of Air India, he took personal interest in even small details that affected the brand image and set very high standards for the quality to be maintained in operations and service. He keenly observed and made elaborate notes on the condition of the planes, quality of food, service, and so on whenever he flew on Air India and instructed the operations team about these. Air India earned a reputation for the exclusive experience it offered to air travellers.

Nationalization

In 1953, the government of India decided to nationalize all private airlines. Accordingly, all existing airlines in the country were nationalized and formed into two companies: Indian Airlines for domestic operations and Air India for international operations. The government requested JRD to serve as the Chairman of Air India. Though he had reservations about the functioning of the airline under government control, he accepted the responsibility of running the airline without any remuneration.

JRD continued to focus on maintaining the identity and reputation that Air India had built over the years.

In February 1978, the government of India discontinued the services of JRD as the Chairman of Air India. Though he was reappointed on the boards of Indian Airlines and Air India in 1980 with a change in the government, this stint lasted only till 1982.[13]

Airline Industry in India

The Government of India, in 1992, opened up the aviation sector (which was till then restricted) to private players. India in the 1990s and 2000s saw the entry of a number of private players in the market. However, many prominent players like Kingfisher Airlines and Jet Airways as well as many smaller players discontinued operations due to continued losses. Other players like Air Deccan were taken over by other airlines. Though the Indian aviation sector exhibited steady growth and promise, most of the operators were under financial strain. This was attributed to the high cost of aviation turbine fuel due to steep taxes in addition to intense competition.[14]

Though during the 1980s–1990s Air India ran international operations successfully, the following decade saw its performance deteriorate. The organization was mostly headed by government-appointed bureaucrats. The liberalization of the aviation industry during the 1990s saw the emergence of new competition. Indian Airlines found it difficult to compete with more agile private players like IndiGo, SpiceJet, and Go Air. Though Air India continued to be profitable, it was merged with the struggling Indian Airlines in 2007.[15] The combined entity saw a steady decline in market share, and by 2020 had accumulated losses of Rs.840 billion.[16]

The government had made attempts to privatize Air India in 2000 and 2017 but had not succeeded because of opposition by unions and since the government wanted to continue to hold a stake in the business.

During the year 2020, the sector handled 340 million passengers in the country, with IndiGo Airlines claiming a market share of 48.2%, followed by SpiceJet with 15.6%, Air India with 10.9%, and GoAir with 10.8%, respectively. Air Asia and Vistara, in which the Tatas had stakes, had a market share of 6.7% and 5.8%, respectively[17] (see Table 2.3).

Tatas Re-enter Airlines Business

Like JRD, Ratan Tata was also passionate about flying and was keen on re-entering the airlines business. The group had made an unsuccessful attempt to start an airline in partnership with Singapore Airlines in 1994. They had also made an attempt to buy a stake in Air India

TABLE 2.3 Major Airlines Operating in India

IndiGo

IndiGo, the market leader in the Indian aviation sector, had a market share of 57% and had a fleet of 285 aircrafts. During the year ended March 31, 2021, it incurred a net loss of Rs.58,064 million.

Air India

Air India was the oldest airline in India. It had a fleet of 128 aircrafts. During the year ended March 31, 2020, it incurred a loss of Rs.77,657 million.

SpiceJet

SpiceJet, the second largest private airline operator in India, had a market share of 8.7% with a fleet of 99 aircrafts. It incurred a loss after tax of Rs.9,983 million during the year ended March 31, 2021.

Vistara

Vistara, a joint venture of Tata Sons with Singapore Airlines Limited (SIA) had a market share of 8.3% and a fleet of 51 aircrafts. During the year ended March 31, 2021, it had a loss of Rs.16,116 million.

GoAir

GoAir, rebranded as GoFirst in May 2021, had a market share of 6.8% with a fleet of 55 aircrafts. During the year ended March 31, 2021, it had a loss of Rs.13,335 million.

Air Asia (India)

Air Asia, a subsidiary of Tata Sons was jointly promoted by Tata Sons and Air Asia Berhad Malaysia. It had a market share of 5.2% with a fleet of 34 aircrafts. During the year ended March 31, 2021, it had a net loss of Rs.15,320 million.

Source: Compiled by the author from secondary sources.

along with Singapore Airlines in 2000, which was later shelved by the government. The group finally re-entered the airlines business with two partnerships: Air Asia India in partnership with Air Asia in 2014 and Vistara in partnership with Singapore Airlines in 2015.

The fall in air travel during 2020 due to the pandemic added to the losses. The two airlines had lost Rs.9,000 million till 2021 since they started operations.[18]

Tatas Win the Bid for Air India

The privatization attempt was revived again in 2020 with the government deciding to sell 100% stake in Air India.[19]

Tatas made a bid for Air India through its wholly owned subsidiary Talace Pvt. Limited for an enterprise value of Rs.180,000 million, including a debt of Rs.153,000 million and Rs.27,000 million cash. The offer by Tatas was around 40% higher than the reserve price and also 19% higher than the bid by a consortium led by Ajay Singh, Chairman of SpiceJet. The balance debt of Air India which was around Rs.615,620 million as at end of August 2021 was to be borne by the government.[20] The Tatas got 100% of the stake in Air India and Air India Express[21] as well as 50% of the stake in Air India SATS Airport Services Private Limited, a ground handling entity which was an equal joint venture between Air India and Singapore Airport Terminal Services Limited[22] (see Table 2.4).

Rebuilding Air India: The Challenges

'It won't be a very easy task. Only advantage is they (Tatas) are paying the price which they think they can manage,' said Tuhin Kanta Pandey, Secretary, Department of Investment and Public Asset Management (DIPAM), Government of India, commenting on Tata's acquisition of Air India.[23] While most of the airlines were incurring huge losses due to the pandemic, Air India had been bleeding to the tune of Rs.200 million every day. Apart from the challenge of cutting down operational expenses, there were cultural issues. The morale of the workforce was not high and the organization faced strong unionization. In addition, experts opined that integration with Air Asia and Vistara was going to be complex since Air Asia was a low-cost airline and Vistara was a full-service carrier, whereas Air India was a mix of both.[24] IndiGo, the market leader in terms of market share had built a reputation for on-time service

TABLE 2.4 Financial Statements of Air India (Stand-alone) for 2019–2020 and 2018–2019: Highlights

	Rupees in Million	
	2019–2020	*2018–2019*
Revenue from operations	277,106	255,660
Other income	8,138	9,218
Total revenue	285,244	264,877
Total expenses	362,902	349,625
Loss before tax	77,657	84,748
Loss after tax	77,657	84,748

Source: airindia.in/annualreport-2019–2020.htm

and high operational efficiency. One of the conditions of the sale was that Tatas cannot retrench employees on Air India for one year. While Air India had a strong brand recall, its image had taken a beating over the years. Tatas would be required to invest substantial money in refurbishing Air India's aircrafts as well as for giving it a facelift. There were also questions if Air India would eat into some of Vistara's routes.

At the same time, Tata was yet to make profits from either Vistara or Air Asia as of 2021.

Looking Ahead

Though Tatas were known for strong governance and professional management, experts felt that managing the integration successfully and navigating the competitive Indian aviation market would require considerable resources and expertise from the group. It was to be seen if Tatas would be able to pull it off successfully. All the stakeholders were watching with interest the group's strategy to manage this major acquisition.

Reflective Questions

1. What do you think are the specific strengths of the Tata Group that would enable it to successfully turn around Air India?
2. What do you think was the rationale for Tatas to acquire Air India given that it was a loss-making entity and there were numerous challenges involved in turning around the airline?
3. India was known to be a tough market for airline companies. What are the critical success factors for Tatas to succeed in this business?

Learning Activities

1. *Group activity 1:* Prepare a roadmap for Tatas to manage their airline business with the three airlines – Air India, Vistara, and Air Asia India, each of these coming with their own distinctive business models and cultures. Prioritize the actions that the group has to take.
2. *Group activity 2:* You are a member of the management committee the Tata Group has set up to recommend the integration strategy for the three airlines. To what extent the group should integrate the three airlines and in what time frame?

Notes

1 1 US$ = 76.09 as of April 2022.
2 'Tatas Regain Airloom', *The Times of India*, October 9, 2021.
3 JRD Tata was an industrialist and Chairman of Tata Group from 1938 to 1988.
4 RM Lala, 'Beyond the Last Blue Mountain', *Penguin Portfolio*, 1992.
5 'Tata Brings Air India Home: Here's the Carrier's 90-Year Journey', *Business Standard*, October 8, 2021.
6 'Why Maharaja Is King', *The Times of India*, October 9, 2021.
7 www.statista.com/statistics/. . .
8 'Plane Sailing for Tatas', *The Times of India*, October 9, 2021.
9 'Expanding an Empire', www.tata.com.
10 www.tatatrusts.org

11 'Tata Group Revenue Tops $100 bn; Profit Slips to Near $5 bn', *Business Today.in*, October 29, 2012.
12 Karachi and Bombay were important port cities in India under the British rule prior to 1947. After independence, Karachi became a part of Pakistan and Bombay became a part of India.
13 RM Lala, 'Beyond the Last Blue Mountain', *Penguin Portfolio*, 1992.
14 Sunny Verma, 'Explained: The Rise and Fall of Private Airlines', https://indianexpress.com, April 20, 2019.
15 Pranjal Pande, 'The History Behind India's Flag Carrier: Air India', https://simpleflying.com/air-india-history, May 3, 2021.
16 'Taxpayers Put in Rs.1.1L Cr Since 09–10', *The Times of India*, October 9, 2021.
17 'Market Share of Airlines Across India in Financial Year 2020, by Passengers Carried', https://statista.com/sttistics/575207.
18 'High on E-Play, Tatas Need to Refuel Aviation Business', *The Times of India*, October 9, 2021.
19 'Air India Privatisation Saga: Time to Stop Burning Public Money', *Deccan Herald*, October 18, 2021.
20 'Tatas Regain Airloom', *The Times of India*, October 9, 2021.
21 Launched as a wholly owned subsidiary of Air India in 2005, Air India Express was the low-cost arm of the company with extensive services to the Middle East.
22 Ravi Sharma, 'Air India: Sold for a Song', accessed November 14, 2021, https://frontline.thehindu.com/the-nation/air-india-sold-to-tata-group-for-a-song/article37255654.ece.
23 '"We Want to Finish the Handover Quickly Because We Are Paying Rs.20 Crore to Run the Airline," says DIPAM Secretary on Privatisation of Air India', October 18, 2021, https://businessinsider.in/business/news/air-india-privatization-saga
24 Nishant Sharma, 'Buying Air India Not Enough for Tata to Take on Indigo', https://bloombergquint.com/amp/business/.

PART III

Localization Strategies of Global Companies

3

CHINA MOBILE IN PAKISTAN

Zong's Vision, Strategy, and Growth

K.B.S. Kumar

Synopsis

Even as a mere ten-year-old in Pakistan's telecom sector, Zong had managed to claim 70% of the 4G market share in the segment as of 2017, making itself the most preferred network in Pakistan. Zong, a 100% subsidiary of the China Mobile Communications Corporation, had entered Pakistan in what was its maiden overseas venture and had emerged as the most successful telecom company in the 3G/4G segment, with a subscriber base of more than 6 million. With a clear vision of leading the digital revolution in Pakistan and an unconventional strategy of paying little attention to profits, Zong's focus was on offering the best products and services at rock bottom prices. With strategies like penetration pricing, product differentiation, and market development, Zong carved out a niche for itself as a company with a customer-centric strategy.

Reinvesting its revenues back into growth and development, Zong gave a clear indication of creating and leading the 4G ecosystem in Pakistan and changing the lives of the people. However, with the tough regulatory conditions, brewing competition, and changing trends in the country, the question was how far Zong's strategy of not worrying about profits and developing the market would be sustainable.

Introduction

Even as a mere ten-year-old in Pakistan's telecom sector, Zong had demonstrated accelerated performance which resulted in its claiming 70% of the market share in the 4G segment by 2017. It emerged as the most preferred network in the Pakistani telecom sector.[1] Zong, a 100% subsidiary of the China Mobile Communications Corporation (China Mobile), had entered the Pakistani telecom sector in 2007 in what was its maiden overseas venture. It successfully withstood the competition to emerge as the most successful telecom company in the 3G/4G segment, with a subscriber base of more than 6 million.[2]

DOI: 10.4324/9781003261155-7

With aggressive strategies like penetration pricing, product differentiation, and market development, Zong's was a tough act to follow for fellow players in Pakistan, and it carved out a niche for itself in the market. By 2017, Zong dominated the 3G/4G segment in Pakistan as the single largest player. The company was keen on leading the 4G ecosystem in Pakistan and changing the lives of the people through various avenues. However, with the tough regulatory conditions, brewing competition, and changing trends, the question was how far Zong's strategy of not prioritizing profits and developing the market would be sustainable.

Cellular Telecom in Pakistan

Cellular mobile services had commenced in Pakistan in the 1990s when two companies, Paktel and PakCom, were awarded cellular mobile telephone licenses. In tandem with the global dynamics of mobile telecom markets, Pakistan's telecom sector also picked up pace in the early 2000s. By 2001, Pakistan's telecom sector comprised four players: Ufone (owned by Pak Telecom Mobile), Mobilink (owned by Pakistan Mobile Communications Limited), Instaphone (owned by Pakcom Ltd), and Paktel (owned by Paktel).

The Pakistan Telecom Authority (PTA) introduced various incentives, which included the Calling Party Pays (CPP)[3] regime, reduction in annual royalty from 1.5% to 0.5% of gross revenue, and a reduction in tax and duties. It also reduced the annual license fee and royalty across services like the Card Payphone, and services like electronic information, e-mail, data communication, non-voice communication, and voice mail.

As a result of these initiatives, the Pakistan telecom sector witnessed a boost. The government's initiatives drew the attention of global players like Telenor and Warid Telecom,[4] who set up their services in Pakistan in 2005. The people of Pakistan were quick to embrace cellular services. The phase between the 1990s and 2004 witnessed a significant surge in the cellular subscriber base. The five years between 1999 and 2004 witnessed an unprecedented growth of 200% in the cellular subscriber base (refer to Table 3.1 for growth in mobile subscriber base).

> By 2004, owing to the government's thrust, the regulatory incentives, emerging technologies, and customers' demands, the Pakistani mobile sector was all set to sail the cellular telecom wave (refer to Table 3.2 for the major players in the Pakistan telecom sector).

TABLE 3.1 Growth in Mobile Subscriber Base

Year	*Mobile Subscribers*	*Growth*
1999	265,614	35.5
2000	306,493	15.4
2001	742,606	142.3
2002	1,698,536	128.7
2003	2,404,400	41.6
2004*	6,556,942	172.7

* Till September.

Source: www.pta.gov.pk

TABLE 3.2 Market Share of Mobile Players in Pakistan in 2004

Company	*Share*
Mobilink	62%
Ufone	21%
Instaphone	9%
Paktel	8%

Source: https://pta.gov.pk/media/industry-analysisreport.pdf

Genesis

While Paktel was an independent venture, Pakcom was jointly owned by M/s Afreen and Millicom International, a Sweden-based telecom company. The joint venture had launched the brand Instaphone, whose performance had surpassed Paktel's within a short period of time. However, the entry of a new player, Mobilink, had proved tough for both Paktel and Instaphone. Mobilink's aggressive strategy, better understanding of the market, and culture of innovation had led to its quick success, leaving Paktel and Instaphone behind.[5]

Towards the end of 2000, Paktel rapidly lost market share to competitors. In November 2000, Millicom acquired a 98.9% equity interest in the ailing Paktel to strengthen its position in the market. The acquisition proved constructive for Millicom. In 2001, Millicom conducted several brand improvements and launched Paktel's prepaid services under the brand name *Tango*. In October 2002, Paktel was further allowed to operate a GSM-based network with the necessary frequencies allotted to it. The licenses for launching GSM were renewed for 15 years for a fee of $291 million. In October 2004, with the frequencies obtained, Paktel launched the GSM network. By March 2005, Paktel had approximately 340,000 GSM subscribers and its network comprised 300 cell sites, covering about 45% of Pakistan's population. By the end of 2005, Paktel had secured a market share of 9%, with the subscriber count increasing at a rate of 100,000 per month.

Even as things were looking good, Paktel had to confront unexpected, adverse developments. Contrary to the initial terms of the license agreement, which allowed the payment of the license fee in instalments, PTA refused to allow Paktel to make a delayed payment of a $29 million as an instalment for the license. Further, PTA also refused Paktel permanent access to part of the frequency spectrum. With business conditions turning sour for Millicom, the company exited Pakistan's telecom market in November 2006, after selling its 88.86% stake in Paktel to China Mobile (refer to Table 3.3 for more details about China Mobile) for $284 million. By May 2007, China Mobile had increased its stake in Paktel to 100% and renamed the company China Mobile Pakistan (CMPak). Buoyed by the acquisition and bullish about the future, CMPak invested $700 million soon after the acquisition and $800 million more in 2008. In April 2008, CMPak was rebranded to Zong. Qian Li (Li) was appointed as the maiden CEO of Zong.[6] Li faced a daunting task ahead as Zong had entered a country whose telecom sector was characterized by high taxes, tough regulations, and difficult market penetration. Coupled with this was the critical law and order situation in the country.

TABLE 3.3 About China Mobile: Zong's Parent Company

- Incorporated in 1997 as China Telecom (Hong Kong) Limited, China Mobile was born from the 1999 break-up of China Telecommunications Corporation
- Chinese state-owned telecommunication corporation with China Mobile's total market value stood at RMB 1.57 trillion
- Operates a GSM network; encompasses all 31 provinces in China and directly administered municipalities in Mainland China and includes Hong Kong
- The world's largest mobile phone operator by total number of subscribers, with over 902 million subscribers as of June 2018
- Controls 70% of the Chinese mobile market; 3G subscribers comprise about 10% of its total subscriber base
- Listed on both the NYSE and the Hong Kong Stock Exchange
- First overseas activity was in 2007 with the purchase of Paktel in Pakistan; Launched the Zong brand in 2008
- In 2003 and again in 2007, China Mobile had provided mobile services on Mount Everest

Source: https://publicopinions.net/china-mobile-china-with-total-assets-of-us-218–864-billion/

Market Strategy

Li's market strategy for Zong was influenced by its parent organization's experiences and lessons in China and Hong Kong. Zong's market strategy was based on customer-centric approach, cost leadership, penetration pricing, and product differentiation.

Cost Leadership

Zong treated cost control and reduction as a strategic imperative. It worked on all the possible components that contributed to cost. It brought the hiring, training, marketing, and advertisement costs under the scanner. All the functional departments focused in unison on cost control and reduction, which in turn helped the company in managing the pricing of its products and services.

Product Differentiation

Though Zong was successful in expanding its customer base, it was still lagging behind Mobilink, Ufone, Telenor, and Warid in market share by subscriber base at the end of 2009 (refer to Table 3.4 for market share by subscriber base).

Most of Zong's strategies were research-driven.[7] Guided by the parent organization, it had been intensely focusing on research and development, with its focus on developing innovative and customer-centric products. Zong focused on distinctness in product diversity and differentiation. By 2011, it offered two broad categories of products – pre- and post-paid packages. Within these two categories, Zong offered a wide variety of products, encompassing diverse purposes and targeting a wide spectrum of customers.

Owing to its popularity, Zong witnessed an accelerated growth in its subscriber base. By April 2009, it had touched about 92 million subscribers in the Pakistan telecom sector. In 2008–2009, Zong stood as the company with the highest number of new subscribers in the sector (refer to Table 3.5 for net addition of subscribers). Between 2010 and 2011, Zong

TABLE 3.4 Pakistan Cellular Telecom Market Share by Subscriber Base

Company	*Share*
Mobilink	30.37%
Telenor	24.82%
Ufone	19.30%
Warid	12.54%
Zong	12.87%

Source: www.scribd.com

TABLE 3.5 Net Addition in Subscribers: April 2009

Company	*Subscribers*
Mobilink	141,637
Ufone	102,006
Telenor	122,168
Warid	135,128
Zong	148,035

Source: www.scribd.com

TABLE 3.6 Zong's Subscriber Base in 2011–2012

Month	*Subscribers*
July 2011	11,594,583
August 2011	12,045,445
September 2011	12,591,110
October 2011	13,168,025
November 2011	13,572,798
December 2011	13,874,709
January 2012	14,423,646
February 2012	14,951,789

Source: Compiled from www.zong.com.pk.

successfully added 3.1 million subscribers to its base, and was declared the fastest growing network in Pakistan. According to PTA's statistics, Zong had significantly expanded its subscriber base during the period January–April 2011, taking its subscriber base from about 13.2 million to about 15 million subscribers by 2012 (refer to Table 3.6 for Zong's subscriber base 2011–2012).[8]

In 2014, in the crowded 3G market, Zong differentiated itself by launching its 'Super 3G' package which was characterized by extremely fast internet, seamless access to data, and best in class technology – HSPA+ (High Speed Packet Access).[9] By 2015, Zong had put up an impressive performance and surged ahead to occupy the second position by subscriber base, next only to Telenor, leaving behind giants such as Mobilink, Ufone, and Warid. By

2015, Zong had claimed as many as 2.9 million 3G subscribers[10] (refer to Table 3.7 for 3G subscribers).

The 4G Wave

The fierce fight in the 2G and 3G segments continued through 2014. Zong was still struggling to retain and capture market share against players like Telenor and Mobilink. In 2014, a sweeping shift was in the offing for the Pakistan telecom sector that went unnoticed by most players in the market. This was the next wave of technology in the telecom sector that threatened to make existing technologies obsolete overnight. It was the 4G wave. Zong was the only player in the Pakistan telecom sector which foresaw the shift and grabbed the first mover advantage, before the competition even woke up to the fact.

Zong faced several regulatory hurdles during the bidding for the spectrum. Nevertheless, it crossed the hurdles. The first hurdle that the regulator introduced during the spectrum bidding was the very high base prices, which were $295 million for the 3G license and $210 million for the 4G license. Second was PTA's pre-condition for the 4G license, that is, making purchase of 10 MHz of 3G spectrum mandatory for a company to qualify for bidding for the 4G license.

Owing largely to these conditions, players like Telenor and Jazz kept away from the bidding. Zong foresaw a promising future in 4G. The experiences of its parent company guided its strategy to take the risk, even as others opted out. Zong emerged as the only telecom player in Pakistan to bid for the 4G spectrum in the 3G/4G auction 2014.

Since then, Zong had been incessantly pumping money into Pakistan's 4G segment. By the end of 2016, Zong's investments in 4G had crossed $300 million and its total investments in the Pakistan telecom sector were in excess of Rs.220 billion.[11] Zong's 4G products were largely based on a detailed process, considering the exact requirements of customers spread across a wide spectrum. Zong borrowed the experience, mechanisms, and models to design products and services from its parent company China Mobile.[12] Liu Dianfeng, who took over as CEO of Zong in November 2014, said that this strategy had enabled the company to provide cutting edge, state-of-the art services to our subscribers. Like its diverse offerings in the 2G and 3G segments, Zong developed 4G products for all types of customers. It brought in differentiation in its offerings, backed by its research-driven culture.

Zong's services offered a combination – quality network, affordable products, and the widest coverage in the nation – which made it the leader in the 4G segment in Pakistan. With its product offerings spread across four categories – prepaid, business, post-paid, and

TABLE 3.7 3G Subscribers: 2015

Company	*Subscribers*
Mobilink	2,860,079
Ufone	2,662,310
Telenor	3,530,421
Zong	2,921,021

Source: https://propakistani.pk/2015/02/02/3g-subscribers-pakistan-reach-6-37-million/

internet – Zong captured all the possible customer segments under its 4G services. Maham Naeem (Naeem), Director Corporate Affairs and Director Strategy, China Mobile Pakistan said, 'Our focus is to expand into, and develop a sustainable 4G ecosystem, profits will follow.'[13]

With advanced services like the fastest internet speed, a wide range of Enterprise Support Solutions, Internet of Things solutions, and Mobile broadband, Zong became the first choice of not only prepaid customers but also corporate and business houses. Zong 4G went on to collaborate with crucial sectors like education, law and order, health, and media to form strong partnerships to offer 4G-based products and solutions. Telenor and Jazz entered the 4G space later on in 2016, but by then Zong had amassed a 4G customer base of 4 million users.

Cultural Transformation

Zong's long-term mission was 'To create and lead the best ecosystem of '4G communication' for every Pakistani to be able to connect anytime, anywhere.' The mission was centred on the idea of enabling a fully connected environment powered by 4G technology. As a part of its cultural change exercise, it defined its core value, which was expected to guide the company's strategy. Zong adopted its core value from its parent organization, China Mobile – 'Responsibility Makes Perfection.'

The management identified five key traits that were thought to be essential to guide Zong towards its vision. The traits were Team Work, Driving Performance, Customer Centricity, Integrity & Accountability, and Innovation. The organization echoed the slogan '*One Company, One Team, One Dream*.' Zong had embraced unconventional methods to recruit resources who believed in contributing to the overall organizational performance, rather than bothering about their own job.

With its pro-employee culture, Zong also touched the personal lives of its employees.

Performance appraisals and feedback were designed around learning rather than indulging in the blame game. Effective designing and implementation of a performance culture had resulted in improved performance, faster turnaround times, and greater productivity. The performance culture had enabled Zong to emerge as a company with the highest performance hikes (up to 81%) and commissions in the sector.

Strategic Alliances

Zong powered its products and innovations with strategic alliances that helped it reach out to the larger customer base spread across various segments. In 2015, it tied up with Pakistan's top courier company, TCS, to offer its mobile broadband devices at TCS's Express Centers located across Pakistan.[14] In 2016, Zong introduced the handset zones at its Customer Services Centers (CSCs) in partnership with Muller & Phipps, the largest distribution company in Pakistan.

The alliance with one of the country's top banks – UBL – enabled UBL credit card customers and UBL employees to access mobile broadband devices (MBB devices) with an upfront purchase of 12 month MBB bundles. A similar tie-up was formed with Silk Bank – a popular banking network.[15]

Zong had joined hands with several major handset makers, namely Huawei, Q-Mobile, Oppo, HTC, and Samsung, Xiaomi,[16] LePhone, and e-commerce platform Daraz.pk. These strategic alliances were effected in light of Zong's vision, '*to develop a complete 4G eco-system in*

TABLE 3.8 3G/4G Subscribers as a Percentage of Total Subscribers in January 2018

Company	*% of 3G/4G Subscribers*
Jazz	31.06%
Zong	46.38%
Telenor	30.03%

Source: Adapted from Pakistan Telecommunication Authority.

the country.' With strategic collaborations and aggressive penetration strategies, by March 2018, it secured a new milestone of 6 million active 4G subscribers across 400 cities[17] (refer to Table 3.8 for 3G/4G subscribers as percent of total subscribers). With a commanding market share of 75% in the 4G segment of the Pakistan telecom sector, Zong looked confident that it would be able to turn its vision for Pakistan into reality.

The Road Ahead

Over the years, Zong had increased its customer base and market share. However, it hadn't made profits even for one quarter since inception. With cost control and penetration pricing at the centre of its strategy to take on the giants of the sector, Zong had focused all its attention on grabbing a share of the market. The dynamics of costs and profits were different between voice and data.

Another significant shift in the communication sector was the rise of the OTT[18] segment, which posed a threat to the telecom companies as it deprived them of revenues. McKinsey & Company's research indicated that the OTTs' share by the end of 2018 could be as high as 60% of messaging and 25% of voice revenues in the Pakistani telecom market.[19]

Amid tough regulatory conditions, brewing competition, and changing trends, the big question was, 'How long would Zong be able to sustain a strategy which paid little attention to profits?'

Reflective Questions

1. Is it sustainable for a company to chase market share at the cost of profits, particularly in a technology- and capital-intensive sector?
2. What do you think are the sectors in which new developments in technology in the telecom sector like 5G would play an important role?

Activities

1. Make teams comprising five to six members each. As an individual, list all possible approaches you can think of for a business player to enter a new geography. Compare your list with those of your team members. Discuss, debate, and come up with the best possible approach for another company like Zong, which is poised to enter the telecom sector of a new market like Pakistan.

2. Draw a Hofstede's cross-cultural analysis of China and Pakistan and discuss with your groups members whether the diversity/differences in the two contexts discussed in the case is/are likely to impact Zong's performance in any way.

Notes

1 Zong Hits More than 6 Million, March 2018, www.techjuice.pk.
2 Ibid.
3 A payment model set basically in cellular mobile market that states that the payment for an incoming call is set on the caller.
4 Warid Telecom International is an Emirati multinational telecommunications company based in Abu Dhabi, United Arab Emirates.
5 Farooq Baloch, 'Recipe for Success: Mobilink Leads with Slogan of Understand, Invest and Innovate', *The Express Tribune*, January 29, 2013, accessed June 15, 2018, https://tribune.com.pk/story/499962/recipe-for-success-mobilink-leads-with-slogan-of-understand-invest-and-innovate/.
6 Mehwish Khan, 'China Mobile Gets New CEO for Zong', *Pro Pakistani*, February 2011, accessed May 5, 2018, https://propakistani.pk/2011/02/22/china-mobile-gets-new-ceo-for-zong/.
7 Adam Kasi, 'Competitive Advantage of Zong', *Competitive Advantage Analysis*, January 16, 2018, accessed September 24, 2018, www.competitiveadvantageanalysis.com/competitive-advantage-of-zong/.
8 "Zong Captures Further Market Share," *Pakistan Today*, June 15, 2011, accessed July 25, 2018, www.pakistantoday.com.pk/2011/06/15/zong-captures-further-market-share.
9 'Zong Launches "Super 3G" in Islamabad', *The Nation*, June 2014, accessed October 25, 2018, https://nation.com.pk/26-Jun-2014/zong-launches-super-3g-in-islamabadwww.nation.com.pk.
10 Saima Ibrahim, 'Telecom Industry 2015 Update: Telenor and Zong Leading the Market', *Phone World*, June 6, 2015, accessed August 25, 2018, www.phoneworld.com.pk/telecom-industry-2015-update-telenor-and-zong-leading-the-market.
11 Parvez Jabri, 'Zong Has Invested over Rs.220 bn to Expand Network', *Business Recorder*, October 3, 2016, accessed July 16, 2018, www.brecorder.com/2016/10/03/321141/zong-has-invested-over-rs220bn-to-expand-network/.
12 '4G Is the Future of Pakistan and Zong 4G Will Make It Happen. Liu Dianfeng, CEO, Zong', *Phone World*, June 26, 2017, accessed July 27, 2018, www.phoneworld.com.pk/4g-is-the-future-of-pakistan-and-zong-4g-will-make-it-happen-liu-dianfeng-ceo-zong/.
13 Farooq Baloch, 'Why "No Profit" Still Makes Zong Happy', *Pakistan Today Profit*, March 5, 2018, accessed September 12, 2018, https://profit.pakistantoday.com.pk/2018/03/05/why-no-profit-still-makes-zong-happy.
14 'Zong MBB Devices Available at TCS Centres', *Pakistan Observer*, March 13, 2016, accessed August 25, 2018, https://pakobserver.net/zong-mbb-devices-available-at-tcs-centres.
15 'Zong to Provide MBB Devices to Silkbank Employees & Customers', *Pro Pakistani*, April 5, 2017, accessed September 24, 2018, https://propakistani.pk/2017/05/04/zong-provide-mbb-devices-silkbank-employees-customers/.
16 A leading Chinese handset maker.
17 'Zong Hits More Than 6 Million Subscribers', *Tech Juice*, March 14, 2018, accessed July 15, 2018, www.techjuice.pk/zong-4g-hits-more-than-6-million-4g-subscribers/.
18 O*TT messaging* is defined as instant *messaging* services or online chat provided by third parties, as an alternative to text *messaging* services.
19 Farooq Baloch, 'Why "No Profit" Still Makes Zong Happy', *Pakistan Today Profit*, March 5, 2018, accessed September 12, 2018, https://profit.pakistantoday.com.pk/2018/03/05/why-no-profit-still-makes-zong-happy/.

4

WHAT'S IN A NAME? STRATEGIC CHALLENGES IN TARGETING AND INTERNATIONAL BRANDING

Glocalization Lessons from a Beer Brand's Market Entry in Nepal

Kranti K. Dugar

Synopsis

Research subjects such as Baburam can provide invaluable insights for marketing mix to companies such as Ullas Breweries Group, especially in foreign markets such as Nepal, where the international marketing task is made more challenging by external uncontrollable sociocultural components. However, in order to do so, companies must commit to a glocalized mindset – bringing global solutions for localized needs/pain points. As a senior marketing researcher found out, the company had problems that led to a key component of a new product in Nepal to be received poorly. His research suggested the targeted market and personas were not perceiving the offering as being acceptable. In fact, fatalism and morbidity were consistently evoked with the brand name Cheetah. The company could learn from its impeding failure so that such mistakes would not be repeated in Asia and elsewhere around the world.

An Escape Mechanism

Where all think alike, no one thinks very much.

–*Walter Lippmann*

Baburam, a porter at the Kathmandu railway station, perceived his life as challenging. He felt increasingly riddled by a sense of despair in a fairly chauvinistic society with demanding responsibility on his shoulders as a breadwinner for a family of six. Nepali was his first language, but over the last five years as a porter/labourer, he had learned to interact in Bhojpuri, Hindi, and Urdu, since many passengers he had to work for spoke those languages. Although he never completed high school, he was observant and perceptive about the political and social uncertainty surrounding him. '*People like me live a life of constant struggle in Kathmandu. There is no upward social mobility. We have been given a raw deal,*'[1] he confided. Exhibiting a

DOI: 10.4324/9781003261155-8

strong sense of hopelessness, he admitted, 'In the current situation, opportunities are limited, resources are few and disturbed, and pessimism is spreading everywhere gradually. Life is a struggle . . . I keep needing to find a reprieve, an escape, even if temporarily.'"[2]

Baburam's despair wasn't limited to social and political unrest. Some of it was a nod to Nepal's quality of life measures. A fairly low male life expectancy at birth of 65 years[3] and a high mortality rate of 681 deaths per 100,000 people,[4] for instance, was not lost on him. His hyper-sensitivity to fatalism (or efforts to escape it, at the least), then, was understandable. Alcoholic beverages, consumed almost every day, were his escape mechanism. Not perceived in the Nepali culture as a social taboo, alcohol was seen as an acceptable social outlet, and more importantly, a welcome diversion or escape mechanism.

> There is a new strong beer on the market. I wanted to give it a try. I did not. It is the devil's drink! Well, I want to escape, but at what cost? It might be deadly! I have mouths to feed, but I might never return home from the bhatti (inconspicuous watering hole)![5]

The Company and Opportunity

The new strong beer Baburam referred to was introduced by Ullas Breweries Group, a global giant with 79 distilleries and bottling units around the world. Commanding a majority share of the Indian spirits market and dominating the Indian brewing market (40% market share), Ullas Breweries Group controlled 60% of the total manufacturing capacity for beer in India and was in a position of advantage in venturing into Nepal with its new offering (an alcoholic non-carbonated beverage slotted for market entry in Kathmandu and, subsequently, in all of Nepal). Bolstered by its success and dominance in other Asian markets and with disregard to marketing research, Ullas froze most elements of its marketing mix (packaging, branding, product attributes, price, and promotion) before it stepped up production. Narang Muni, Chief Marketing Officer of South Asian Operations, was at the helm of the decision to freeze the offering's marketing mix. He had unilaterally decided on those components. So much so that hiring the services of Blue Intelligence Consulting Group, a global marketing intelligence firm, seemed like an afterthought. It was just something that was done as standard practice in the industry. Pratap Raj, Senior Marketing Research Executive, Blue Intelligence, was in-charge of heading the study. He had mixed feelings. He candidly opined,

> We have been hired to conduct marketing mix evaluation and product test studies. On paper, we might fine-tune marketing mix components. However, Ullas is ready to roll and has made heavy investments in production and packaging already. The offering will be exported into Nepal across the border from India. Time is of essence. The elements are frozen, and quite literally at that, because it is March. Cold out here in Kathmandu![6]

It was set then – Ullas would draw on successes in other South Asian markets, brand its offering 'Cheetah' (something that is fast, energetic, exciting, and gets one buzzed/intoxicated quick), and target a demographic profile in Nepal consisting males between 22 and 30 years of age, making less than Nepali Rupees 12,000 ($162)[7] a month, speakers of Nepali, Maithili, Urdu, or Bhojpuri, and belonging in the socio-economic classifications (SEC) of D and E (see Table 4.1). With a concept that translated from Nepali to English as 'Cheetah is a new refreshing strong beer with approximately 8% alcohol strength. This ready-to-drink

TABLE 4.1 SEC Grid for Household Classification in Nepal

CWE – *Occupation code* / CWE –*Education Code*		*Unskilled Workers*	*Skilled Workers*	*Petty Traders*	*Shopowners*	*Businessmen/ Industrialist with Number of Employees*			*Self-employed Professional*	*Clerical/ Salesman*	*Supervisory Level*	*Officers/ Executives – Junior*	*Officers/ Executives – Middle/ Senior*
						None	1–9	10+					
		1	2	3	4	5	6	7	8	9	A	B	C
Illiterate	1	E2	E2	E2	D	D	C	B1	D	D	D	C	B1
Literate but no formal education	2	E2	E1	D	D	C	B2	B1	D	D	D	C	B1
School up to four years	3	E2	E1	D	D	C	B2	B1	D	D	D	C	B1
School five to nine years	4	E1	D	D	C	B2	B2	A2	D	D	C	C	B1
School SSC/HSC	5	D	C	C	B2	B1	B1	A2	B2	C	C	B2	B1
Some college but not a graduate	6	D	C	C	B1	A2	A2	A1	B1	B2	B2	B1	A2
Graduate/postgraduate general	7	D	B2	B2	A2	A2	A1	A1	A2	B1	B1	A2	A1
Graduate/postgraduate – professional	8	D	B2	B2	A2	A1	A1	A1	A1	B1	A2	A2	A1

Source: Compiled by the author.

product from Ullas Breweries Ltd. (Nepal) will leave you feeling nice and high. Priced at just Nepali Rupees 35 for 330 ml' (see Figure 4.1), men like Baburam fit the targeted persona – someone who considered drinking a part of his everyday routine, drank liquor (hard as well as beer) at least three to four times a week, consumed cheap whiskies, rums, and other cheap liquors that cost around Nepali Rupees 40 (about 54 cents) a bottle, and one who aspired a quick buzz, someone open to stronger drink options, someone looking for an escape. Pratap was cautiously optimistic. Ullas was looking at the promise of large-scale potential. Nepal had a population of about 30 million, 1.5 million of whom lived in Kathmandu. About 81% of the population lived in semi-urban or rural parts of Nepal[8] and fit the targeted demographic profile. They had done it in other Asian markets before. Pratap, however, knew that there could be surprises in store, especially since the stakes were so high. How could Ullas be so sure they had the offering right? Had they jumped the gun? Pratap hoped not.

The Pleasant Promise

Pratap designed a mixed method study to evaluate the marketing mix for Cheetah. The qualitative phase would entail focus groups to ascertain acceptance levels for product/concept, packaging format, and price, and the quantitative phase would help evaluate elements of packaging, branding, and communication cues. Secretly, since most elements were frozen and Ullas was committed to market entry into Nepal, Pratap was hoping the offering would be accepted well in its original form. After all, Muni had, in his brief, said, 'Nepal is just across the northeast border from India. Both geographical and cultural distances are low. How different can the needs be? We've got this.'[9]

If one were to go by initial evaluations of the concept, image, price, packaging, and blind evaluations of the product and intentions to purchase, one would have to agree with Muni. The concept, by and large, evoked a strong drink that could get one intoxicated fast and for less. In a sample of 154, 61% respondents reported no dislikes about the concept. The key message the concept was conveying was as follows: The product was *affordable, novel, strong, energetic, refreshing, appealing, relevant, believable,* and *unique*. The image of the offering was

चीता एउटा नया, ताजा र आठ प्रतिशत
मदिरा भ्येको कड़ा बीयर हो।
यो यु.बी. नेपाल को तैयार पेय
ले हजूर लायी बढ़िया र स्फूर्तिदायक
अनुभव दिने छ। यो बीयर केवल रु.३५
मा उपलब्ध छ।

FIGURE 4.1 Product concept of Cheetah in Nepali.

Source: Primary source.

evaluated as being innovative and distinctive. About 68% respondents evaluated the price point as being just right. In a blind test, the top-two box score for intention to buy (definitely/probably buy) was a whopping 96%, with a mean score of 4.60 (on a 5-point scale). A green bottle was preferred over clear and brown bottles (see Figure 4.2). The top-two box score for likeability of label design was 92%, with a mean score of 4.40. Blind product evaluations (post-drink) indicated words/phrases such as *unique, sweet, appealing, low on fizziness, high on drinkability, intoxicating after two to three drinks* (strength was established unambiguously), and *non-lingering smell*. Top-of-the-mind likes about the product were reported as follows: *taste* (47%), *colour* (27%), and *sweetness* (25%). About 60% respondents reported no dislikes about the product post-drink. The top-two box score for product likeability post-drink (in a blind taste test) was 97%, with a mean score of 4.63. The just-right scores for top product attributes were high too (80% for colour, 77% for sweetness, 81% for bitterness, 80% for thickness, 78% for strength, 85% for flavour, and 68% for price). Overall product evaluations pre-drink were fairly high, but improved significantly post-drink (see Figure 4.3). The top-two box score for intention to buy (blind test) post-drink (definitely/probably buy) was again a whopping 96%, with a mean score of 4.60.79% respondents reported a desire to consume the product three to four times a week (65% reported they'd drink two to three bottles per occasion). About 90% respondents said they'd switch beer brands to consume this new offering. Breathing a sigh of relief, Pratap was looking forward to presenting his findings to Muni at Ullas. Most of Pratap's work was done. With only non-blind tests for label design and brand name evaluations to

FIGURE 4.2 Three Cheetah bottles tested (brown, green, and clear).

Source: Created by the author.

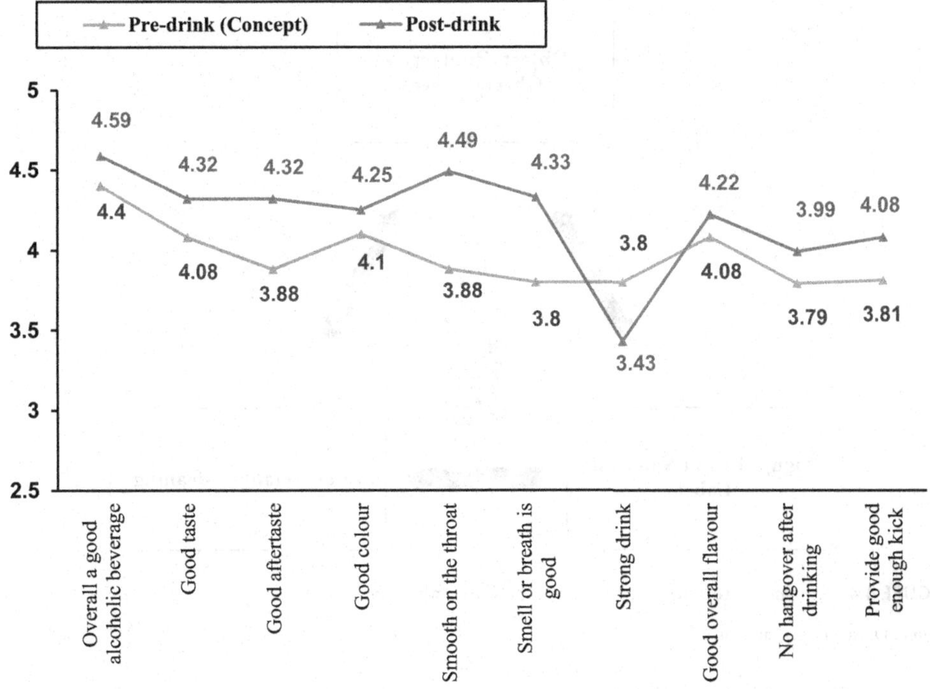

FIGURE 4.3 Product evaluation scores: pre- and post-drink (n = 154) – 5-point Likert scale.

Source: Created by the author.

conduct the following day, he consumed two bottles of cold Cheetah beer supplied by the client and went to bed happy and content.

The (Unpleasant) Discovery

The next morning, in a non-blind label test and brand name evaluation test, Pratap discovered something unpleasant. A proud graduate of a top MBA school in India, Pratap took pride in his brand-related intelligence work and drew from his vast experience. He swore by concepts such as semiotics and brand intimacy and used them consistently to understand the use of signs and symbols to create meaning.[10] He knew that in semiotics, an object was the product that was the focus of the message (e.g. Cheetah beer), the sign was the sensory stimulus or image that represented the intended meanings and perceptions of the object (e.g. the Cheetah label and brand name), and the interpretant was the meaning prospective/targeted consumers would derive from the sign (e.g. a desirable, affordable, strong, new beer). For the sake of his Cheetah study, he was counting on these three components to be aligned and in sync (see Figure 4.4). He also knew beverage brands that had easy access to olfactory and other sensory outlets, could form intimate and deeply emotional bonds with prospective users.[11] What's more, he had designed the study with an eye specifically on the target market that fit an adapted version of the 4 A's Model of serving low-income, bottom-of-the-pyramid (BOP)[12] customers (see Figure 4.5).[13,14]

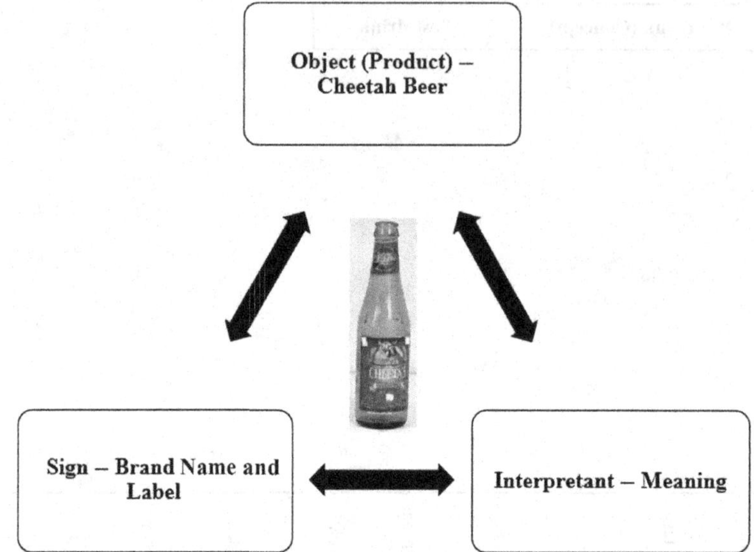

FIGURE 4.4 Semiotic relationships specific to Cheetah beer.

Source: Drawn by the author.

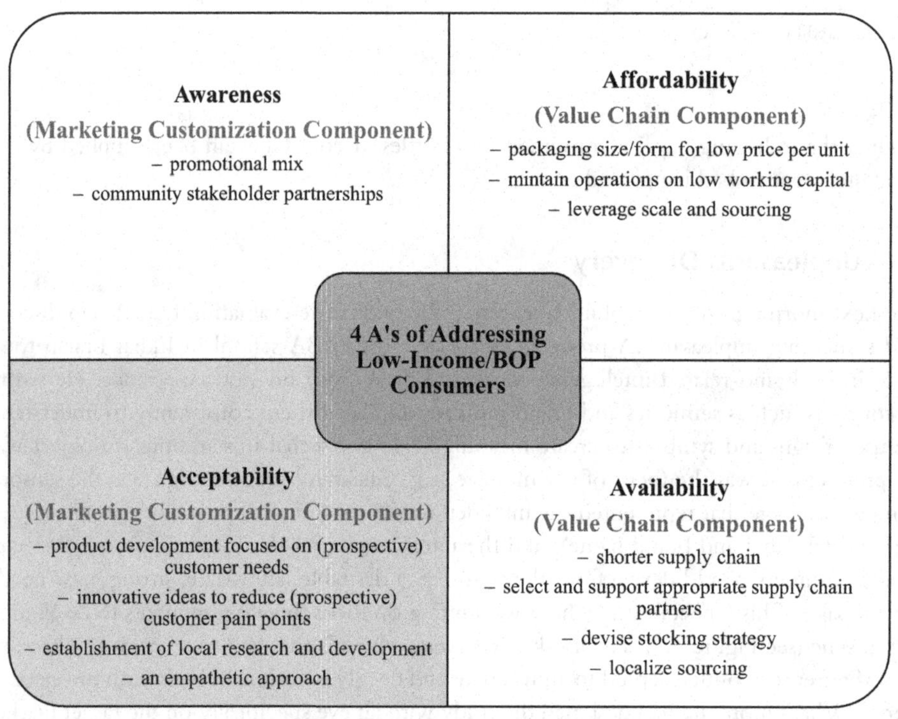

FIGURE 4.5 The 4 A's model of addressing low-income consumers.

Source: Adapted by the author from the 4 A's model of addressing low-income consumers (from Anderson & Billou, 2007; Kearney, 2007).

He had left no stone unturned. However, respondents' evaluations that morning hit him like rocks and brickbats. The image of the wild animal (cheetah) on the label was not registering with the respondents. They perceived it to be a different animal and as *not at all attractive* and *energetic*. 'A cheetah is full of aggression and energy. . . . [T]his one looks hungry and dull,' said one respondent.[15] It was almost as if they didn't want to see the cheetah on the label. Most respondents, who were speakers of Nepali, Maithili, or Bhojpuri, expressed shock at the brand name. Through a Brand Association Perceptual Map (Associative Network), a visual representation of the attributes and concepts associated with the brand, it was discovered that the brand name was evoking a despairing sense of morbidity and fatalism. Words/phrases such as *danger*, *fear*, *last stage of human life*, *dead body*, *death*, and *funeral pyre* were evoked repeatedly. The bottom-two box score for likeability of the brand name (dislike it very much/dislike it somewhat) was a hugely concerning 86%, with a mean score of just 1.34 (on a 5-point scale). Further, on evaluations of 'suitability of brand name with product concept,' respondents reported a mean score of a mere 1.62 (on a 5-point scale).

It was becoming clear to Pratap that there was intense disagreement between object, sign, and interpretant components with this offering's brand name, and the cultural meaning-making evoked by the respondents pointed to a serious semiotic flaw – something that would need much more than just fine-tuning. This was unprecedented. For the life of him, Pratap could not understand the invocation of fatalism. It was throwing him for a loop! He knew there could be no yea-saying at the client presentation. This offering, in its current form, was destined to fail in Nepal. Factors of production were in motion. Expectations were high. What would he report to Muni, and how?

A Moment of Reckoning

Fall seven times, stand up eight.

–Japanese proverb

Local voices such as Baburam's had the potential to enable companies like Ullas Breweries Group to draw from glocal (global and local) intelligence and offer products aligned with target market persona(s). It was ironic that the voice came from a study that was almost an afterthought. Since Pratap's company had had Ullas as a client for so many years, he decided he had to point out problems stemming from top-down decision-making and a company culture encouraging high-power distance,[16] where groupthink could be prevalent. Was company culture to blame for this impending failure in market entry into Nepal? Had Ullas Breweries Group (and Mr. Muni) been ethnocentric in rolling out their offering and international marketing mix of Cheetah? Why was the brand name Cheetah invoking such morbid meanings? What components of the Model had Ullas overlooked (especially the *acceptability* component)? What lessons about marketing strategy could Ullas Breweries Group learn from this impending failure? Pratap knew there could be no easy answers.

Thought Questions

Thought Questions: International Marketing

1. Why was the brand name Cheetah invoking such morbid meanings in Nepal and what was the semiotic disconnect in branding it as such?

2. What Ullas Breweries Group could have done differently in its market entry and marketing mix strategy in Nepal as it relates to ethnocentrism and the 4 A's Model?
3. How would you diagnose gaps in segmentation, targeting, and positioning that kept the offering from presenting effective marketing mix aligned with needs in Nepal?

Thought Questions: Strategic Management

1. Why was the brand name Cheetah invoking such morbid meanings in Nepal and what was the semiotic disconnect in branding it as such?
2. How does the groupthink model apply to this case?
3. How does company culture and power distance apply to this case?

Notes

1 Personal interview with author, March 20, 2004, Kathmandu, Nepal.
2 Ibid.
3 United Nations, Department of Economic and Social Affairs, Population Division (2019). World Population Prospects 2019: Data Booklet. ST/ESA/SER. A/424.
4 World Population Prospects 2022: Demographic indicators by region, subregion and country, annually for 1950–2100. population.un.org. United Nations Department of Economic and Social Affairs, Population Division. Retrieved September 17, 2022.
5 Personal interview with author, March 20, 2004, Kathmandu, Nepal.
6 Personal interview with author, February 19, 2004, Bangalore, Karnataka, India.
7 'NPR to USD Historical Chart 2004', *Exchange Rates*, n.d., accessed August 24, 2022, https://exchangerates.org/npr/usd/in-2004.
8 'Nepal Demographics Profile 2004', *CIA World Factbook*, accessed August 19, 2022, www.cia.gov/the-world-factbook/countries/nepal/.
9 Personal interview with author, February 19, 2004, Bangalore, Karnataka, India.
10 MR Solomon, 'Perception: Semiotics: The Meaning of Meaning', in *Consumer Behavior: Buying, Having, and Being* (pp. 96–98). Essay, Pearson Education, Inc.: Hoboken, NJ, 2020.
11 M Natarelli and R Plapler, 'Theory & Model', in *Brand Intimacy: A New Paradigm in Marketing* (pp. 91–97). Essay, Hatherleigh Press: New York, 2017.
12 CK Prahalad, *The Fortune at the Bottom of the Pyramid: Eradicating Poverty Through Profits*. Prentice Hall, India, 2014.
13 J Anderson and N Billou, 'Serving the World's Poor: Innovation at the Base of the Economic Pyramid', *Journal of Business Strategy, 28*(2) (2007), 14–21.
14 AT Kearney, 'Serving the Low-Income Consumer: How to Tackle This Mostly Ignored Market', *Executive Agenda, 51* (2007), 49–57.
15 Personal interview with author, February 19, 2004, Bangalore, Karnataka, India.
16 G Hofstede, GJ Hofstede, and M Minkov, *Cultures and Organizations: Software of the Mind* (3rd ed.). McGraw-Hill, New York, 2010.

PART IV
Strategic Challenges

5

HDFC BANK

Can It Overcome Technology Issues and Get Back on Growth Track?

Sanjay Fuloria

Synopsis

Starting in December 2018, HDFC Bank Limited, the first and the leading private sector bank in India faced serious problems in its technology infrastructure leading to large-scale disruptions in its online services. Being at the forefront of digitization, for HDFC Bank, this was a serious setback. It had to face strictures and imposition of restrictions by the Reserve Bank of India on launching new digital initiatives and issue of new credit cards. This halted its aggressive growth in the highly competitive credit card business. The investigations into the problem revealed lapses in the way the technology infrastructure was managed by the bank. The infrastructure had not kept pace with the growth of business of the bank. The bank had to find short- and long-term strategies to ensure such instances were not repeated again.

Introduction

In June 2021, Sashi Jagdishan (Jagdishan), the Managing Director and CEO of India-based private sector bank HDFC Bank Limited (HDFC Bank), said 'In the last couple of years our technological capability has been questioned, justifiably.'[1] This statement coming from the head of a behemoth like HDFC Bank did not speak too well about the brand. HDFC Bank was the first private sector bank in India. It was set up in 1994. In 2021, it had 5,779 branches and 17,238 ATMs in 2,956 cities and towns.[2] In the October–December quarter of 2021, HDFC Bank reported a net profit of Rs.103.42 billion.[3,4] HDFC Bank's nearest rival ICICI Bank had a net profit of Rs.61.94 billion in the same quarter.[5] However, ICICI Bank had made very good progress in using technology in the business and had also been able to adopt technology smoothly in its operations without much trouble. Where did HDFC Bank go wrong?

DOI: 10.4324/9781003261155-10

Issues

On November 21, 2018, HDFC Bank's customers were not able to make online transactions. Nothing was working – internet banking, UPI,[6] or mobile banking. The systems in the bank for in-person banking were working though. As complaints started piling up, the bank realized the problem was in the data centre located at Navi Mumbai.[7] The data centre was down because the power bills were not paid, and the electricity supply was cut off. Data centres relied heavily on uninterrupted power supply. Despite the backup systems,[8] the data centre of HDFC went down.[9]

Glitches in Going Digital

HDFC Bank positioned itself as a digital bank. Lack of sufficient investments in Information Technology was cited as one of the reasons for all the technical glitches like obsolete technology, and power issues that the bank faced. While the bank's business was expanding, the IT Infrastructure was not upgraded. Another situation was a purported cyberattack in December 2019 that generated extraordinary traffic to the bank's website resulting in downtime. The bank avoided hiring external consultants for digital initiatives to control spending and had instead set up in-house IT systems.

HDFC Bank started its digital journey in 2014. Aditya Puri, the then Managing Director and CEO, wanted HDFC Bank to be disruptive before a competitor did that. The bank had set specific targets to apply artificial intelligence to improve the bank's functioning, to revolutionize marketing procedures, and reduce turnaround times. The bank was proud of their target-based approach. The start was good but as the saying goes, 'the road to hell is paved with good intentions.' Whenever there were technical glitches, the management used to bury the issues by making flowery PowerPoint presentations. Even the data centre was not owned by HDFC Bank but by Reliance Communications. Some outages at the data centre were tied to the failure of air-conditioning at the data centre in Navi Mumbai. As a result of these outages, in December 2020, the Reserve Bank of India (RBI) put a temporary hold on HDFC Bank from launching new digital banking initiatives and issuing new credit cards.

HDFC Bank decided to set up a contemporary digital customer experience centre in 2022 that allowed information to be accessed across channels and devices. The digital experience of consumers was a top priority for them; thus, they redesigned their payment options. To further enhance their IT infrastructure, the bank implemented several measures. Key objectives included doubling the capacity for UPI, doubling the capacity for net banking and mobile banking to support 90,000 concurrent users, a big step, as most of the clients relied on digital channels and devices for financial purposes.

Technology

Data centres in Bangalore and Mumbai were upgraded to the latest technology by the bank after facing problems in 2021. With Disaster Recovery (DR) automation and the adoption of hot DR active asset setup[10] for key applications, the bank advanced to the next level of disaster recovery. In hot DR active asset set-up, order application and associated services were deployed in two data centres; however, traffic was routed to an active data centre only when there were problems with the primary data centre. The hot standby data centre was ready to be activated in the event of a disaster in the primary data centre. All that was needed to implement a disaster recovery plan was a simple change in the load balancer configuration. While the second data centre was operational and up to date, the application was not used to process customer requests in hot standby mode. Both data centres were covered by the same software license, even if only one was now operational. Massive network and security infrastructure changes were required to keep pace with the exponential rise in the volume of digital transactions.[11] In the typical retail product, for example, close to 80% of new loans were underwritten using digital scorecards or automated underwriting systems. Digital score cards were created by analysing the delinquency patterns and income levels of the individuals.

The traditional banking paradigm relied on branches, employees, and customer loyalty. The new paradigm could not leave out technology. For example, post-pandemic work-from-home was driving banks to rethink their office space and productivity.[12] There were significant setbacks on the manpower front for the bank when it came to the digital leadership team. They lost senior people to competition. In addition to cultivating and hiring digital banking talent, HDFC Bank would also need to pay equal attention to cyber security and data protection, which would be at the forefront in a fully-fledged digital banking market. There were plenty of problems for HDFC Bank to solve.

Reflective Questions

1. When do corporate-level initiatives related to technology work? When do they not work?
2. How do you create a system to ensure that different functions and departments in organizations work in sync with each other?
3. Do you think extensive use of technology increases the vulnerability of an organization to disruptions?

Activities

1. Visit a bank and identify the areas in its operations where digitization is playing a role.
2. Design and conduct a survey of the customers of a bank to assess their tolerance to disruption in online access.

Notes

1 '"Redoubled Efforts to Fix Issue": HDFC Bank CEO Apologises for Tech Outages', June 24, 2021, www.businesstoday.in, June 24, 2021.
2 'Company History – HDFC Bank Ltd.', https://economictimes.indiatimes.com/hdfc-bank-ltd/infocompanyhistory/companyid-9195.cms.
3 'Audited Standalone Financial Results for the Quarter and Year Ended March 31, 2022', www.hdfcbank.com/content/.
4 In December 2021, the exchange rate was 1 US$ = INR75.79.
5 'ICICI Bank's Net Profit Rises 25 Per Cent to ₹6,194 Crore', www.hindustantimes.com/business/icici-bank-net-profit-rises-25-per-cent-to-rs-6–194-crore-101642852406401.html.
6 Unified Payments System, a real-time, online payment system.
7 Navi Mumbai or New Bombay is a satellite township on the western suburbs of Bombay.
8 Typically, if the power goes out, a UPS system takes over. If the power does not get restored in 15 minutes, diesel generators keep the power supply going.
9 'Sorry for the Inconvenience: Why Your Bank's Systems Keep Failing', https://the-ken.com/story/sorry-for-the-inconvenience-why-your-banks-systems-keep-failing/?searchTerm=HDFC%20Bank.

10 It is an active standby topology to minimize interruptions.
11 Shayan Ghosh and Gopika Gopakumar, 'Inside HDFC Bank's Digital Stumble', www.livemint.com/industry/banking/inside-hdfc-bank-s-digital-dilemma-11620747000595.html.
12 Anand Adhikari, '5 Big Challenges for New HDFC Bank CEO Sashidhar Jagdishan', www.businesstoday.in/latest/corporate/story/5-big-challenges-for-new-hdfc-bank-ceo-sashidhar-jagdishan-269105-2020-08-04.

6

INDIA POST PAYMENTS BANK

Postal Services to Banking – Will the Journey Be Smooth?

R. Bala Subramanian, N. Manjula, and G.V. Muralidhara

Synopsis

India Post, one of the oldest organizations in India provided postal services through its extensive network of post offices throughout the country. It had earned a name for trust and reliability and was the only service available for communication in remote parts of the country. In 2018, it launched the India Post Payments Bank to provide banking services through the post offices. India Post had been offering postal services at an affordable price to the customers, which resulted in a revenue deficit requiring regular financial support by the government. The organization was run like a government department. On the other hand, India Payments Bank had to compete against existing, well-established banks. The organization had to transform itself to succeed in the new business. Given its legacy as a government institution, it was going to be a huge challenge for it to compete in a dynamic industry like banking.

Introduction

On September 1, 2018, Narendra Modi (Modi), the prime minister of India, launched the payments bank of the department of posts with the aim of providing banking services to a large section of the Indian population who had no access to banking.[1]

The India Post Payments Bank (IPPB), initially operational at 650 branches and 3,250 access points, was expected to quickly scale to 0.155 million post offices, with 0.13 million of these located in rural areas. For the department of posts, which already offered postal savings bank to 170 million account holders, this was an opportunity to contribute to financial inclusion in the country in a big way through the use of technology.

Indian Post was one of the oldest organizations in the country. Starting with the opening of the first post office in Calcutta in 1727 and the subsequent opening of Calcutta GPO on March 31, 1774, during British rule, it had become the most important channel of

DOI: 10.4324/9781003261155-11

communication between people located in different corners of the country. From a network of 23,344 post offices, mainly in urban areas at the time of independence in 1947, the network had expanded to 154,965 post offices by 2017, becoming the largest postal network in the world. With 139,067 post offices located in rural areas, the Indian postal service connected most interior parts of the country.[2]

In 2020, India stood at the fourth position, with a score of 56.14 on the ranking based on the Integrated Index for Postal Development (2IPD) of the Universal Postal Union. This indicated an upper-intermediate level of performance belonging to the top 50% of countries.[3]

Over the years, the organization had introduced several services, including telegram, money order, speed post courier service, and post office savings schemes. However, after the widespread use of the internet and electronic mail from the 1990s, the traditional postal services were gradually losing relevance and postal services of different countries were reinventing their business models to stay relevant. In 2015, the Reserve Bank of India (RBI) announced the licensing of differentiated banking services – small finance and Payments Bank. A Payments Bank operated like any other bank operating on a smaller scale accepting demand deposits up to Rs.0.1 million, offering remittance services, utility bill payments, mobile payments/transfers, direct benefit transfers, and third-party fund transfers but without any lending activities or issue of credit cards.[4]

There were several challenges IPPB had to overcome to succeed. With the legacy of a government institution, it had to shed the bureaucracy to compete in a dynamic industry like banking. The stringent norms of the RBI would make it difficult for IPPB to create a profitable business model. India Post had a revenue deficit of Rs.119,690 million in 2016–2017.[5]

Experts pointed out that IPPB can make a difference if it was run as a business entity and not as a government department. Technology would play a key role in its success, they pointed out. While recognizing the role of a postman who was a familiar figure among the households, they opined that love for the postman alone cannot make IPPB a success and it needed to do much more.[6]

History of Postal Services in India

The foundation of the organized postal system in India was laid in 1688 with the launch of the first post office by the British in Bombay. In 1727, a post office was opened in Calcutta. In 1774, the Calcutta GPO (General Post Office) was established. In 1786, the Madras GPO was established. In 1837, through an ordinance, the government took absolute control of the postal system. In subsequent years, the British expanded the postal network to more places. The focus of expansion was mainly on strategic and trade reasons. At the time of independence and partition in 1947,[7] there were 136,591 employees in the Posts and Telegraphs Department. During the partition, 26,284 employees went to Pakistan postal department. The number of employees in the department went up to 6,77,0000 in 1976 and 608,904 in 1984. In 1984, the Posts and Telegraphs Department was divided into Posts and Telecommunications departments. Over the years, the postal department established a name for trust. The postman was a familiar figure in villages and remote places where post offices were the only means of communication. With the facilities of postal savings accounts and postal life insurance, post offices became places where the citizens could avail multiple services at a single location. Post-independence, the emphasis was on inclusion and thus the network expanded into all corners of the country.[8]

Growth of India Post

India Post introduced new products and services regularly and also expanded its reach to touch people in different corners of the country (see Figure 6.1 for important milestones in India Post's journey).

In 1947, there were 23,344 post offices across the country, of which 19,184 were in rural areas, and the balance were in urban areas. Starting with the popular and economical postcard in 1879, inland letters were introduced subsequently, followed by Speed Post in 1986 and then the e-post. In 1930, postal orders were introduced. The system of using a pin code similar to a zip code was introduced in 1972. In 1977, the department introduced a new product Value Payable Post, parcels and insured parcels. In 1984, the department was divided into two separate divisions, namely the Department of Posts and the Department of Telecommunications. In 1994, satellite-based money order service was introduced. The department initiated several projects to bring about improvements in the services provided. Project Arrow was initiated in 2008 to create an effective, friendly environment for staff and customers. A postal savings plan was also introduced. A Mail Network Optimization Plan (MNOP) was initiated in 2010 to improve the quality of mail operations through consolidation and optimization of the mail network. Around 27,200 post offices and administrative offices were linked through a wide area network (WAN). In keeping with the demand for faster deliveries and to develop corporate business, services like express parcel, business parcel, cash on delivery, online money transfer service, instant money order, and e-greeting were added. GPS-enabled logistics and postal delivery through GIS mapping were introduced in 2009. The Mobile Money Transfer facility was introduced in 2012 to facilitate instant transfer from one place to another using a mobile network. By 2017, the network of post offices in the country had reached 154,965, with 139,067 of these being in rural areas, with one post office serving 7,753 people on average.[9]

Postal Services in the Internet Age

The advent of the internet during the 1990s in providing an alternate means of communication and the entry of mobile phones during the 2000s created a huge dent in the volume of mail traffic of India Post. From a mail traffic of 15,749 million in 1997–1998, the volume fell to 6,677 million in 2006–2007, and 6,391 million in 2007–2008, which rose marginally to 6,541 million in 2008–2009. In 2016–2017, the mail traffic was 6,189 million. The number of post offices also came down marginally from 155,204 to 1,54,965 in 2016–2017.[10]

Postal Savings Account

India Post offered various small savings schemes from 1882. The schemes offered as part of this were savings account, recurring deposit, time deposit, monthly income account scheme, public provident fund, and national savings certificates, among others. The department took up an IT modernization project in 2012 to enable customers to avail of 'Anywhere Anytime Banking,' and other facilities like net banking, NEFT, and RTGS. Automated Teller Machines (ATMs) were also made available to withdraw money anytime. The department also offered postal insurance to some segments of the population.[11]

Payments Bank

The Nachiket Mor Committee on Comprehensive Financial Services for Small Businesses and Low-Income Households,[12] in its report released in January 2014, recommended issuing licenses for setting up Payments Banks. The Finance Minister of India announced that RBI would create a framework for licensing small banks and other differentiated banks to meet the credit and remittance needs of small businesses, unorganized sectors, low-income households, farmers, and the migrant workforce. Subsequently, in 2015, RBI issued guidelines for the issue of licenses for Payments Banks as differentiated or restricted banks.

According to these guidelines, Payments Banks were permitted to accept demand deposits, that is, current deposits and savings bank deposits, provide payments and remittance services, offer internet banking, and function as Business Correspondent (BC) of other banks. They were not allowed to set up subsidiaries to undertake non-banking financial service activities. The Payments Banks were not allowed to undertake lending activities and were required to invest in government securities and treasury bills. As these banks were required to invest heavily in technological infrastructure, they were required to have a minimum paid-up equity capital of Rs.1,000 million.[13]

India Post Payments Bank

On September 1, 2018, the prime minister of India launched the India Payments Bank with the aim of converting the vast network of post offices in the country into banking access points, giving a fillip to financial inclusion in the country. The government provided a budget of Rs.14.35 billion to the department to set up the bank. Of the entities the RBI had issued licenses in 2015 to set up payments banks, only three banks – Paytm, Airtel, and Fino – were running operations for more than six months by 2018. Apart from 650 branches that were already operational, IPPB planned to convert 155,000 post offices as access points, making its network more than three times the number of branches operated by all scheduled commercial banks in the country. It planned to train its 3,00,000 postmen in banking operations and digital operations. IPPB planned to charge a fee of Rs.25 plus GST per transaction for providing doorstep facilities to its customers. Other non-financial transactions provided at the doorstep were also chargeable. (see Table 6.1 for a summary of the facilities provided by IPPB). Payments for the services were the main source of revenue for IPPB as it was not permitted to lend money or issue credit cards. As urban citizens had the option of opening accounts with regular banks that provided many facilities, they were not likely to patronize IPPB. Citizens in rural areas were likely to use these facilities. However, many of them already had access to a zero-balance facility with regular banks through the Jan Dhan Yojana, which the government implemented in 2014.[14] IPPB was planning to link the 170,000 existing savings accounts to the payments bank. As there was a limit of Rs.100,000 for deposits in the payments bank, it provided a facility or sweep-in of the amounts to the linked postal savings accounts. In the first year of operation, IPPB had reached a customer base of 10 million[15] and by January 2022, it had reached 50 million customers, with 48% of these being women.[16] In 2022, the government provided additional funding of Rs.8,200 million to IPPB to help it expand its operations deeper into the country.[17]

Challenges

The department of posts had been incurring losses every year in its operations. Critics questioned how an organization that was inefficient and losing money on every service it provided could be successful in running a bank that required dynamic working and faster decision-making. Since it operated as a department of the government, it was subject to the bureaucracy that was typical of a government set-up. They also questioned its business model. They opined that payment banks were not a viable and sustainable business model since they were not allowed to lend and they were also required to invest most of the amount collected as deposits in government securities. The only source of revenue was the charges for the services rendered to its customers. Since IPPB operated with physical branches and correspondents, the cost of operation was high. Experts pointed out that payments banking was a low-margin activity.[18] To create other revenue streams IPPB planned to offer loans, mutual funds, and insurance through third-party tie-ups.

The Road Ahead

Since its launch in 2018, IPPB had opened more than 52 million accounts and carried out 820 million transactions with a value of Rs.1,618 billion.[19] With its background of running a postal service with a wide network across the country and also managing a large number of postal savings accounts, IPPB had a head start. It had the advantage to reach, access, and credibility among the rural population. But with the legacy of a traditional business, record of losses, cost of operations, and the inherent non-viability of payment banks as a business model, the jury on whether IPPB will achieve financial inclusion along with profitability was still open.[20]

Reflective Questions

1. Discuss the challenges India Post Payments Bank faces in transitioning from delivering posts to delivering banking services.
2. Create a roadmap for India Post Payments Bank to create a technology-driven, agile, and efficient organization capable of operating successfully in the dynamic banking industry.

Activities

1. Visit a post office in your area and observe the processes that are followed. Note down the important attributes of people working in post offices.
2. Based on your observation, prepare a report on the important characteristics of a post office operation.
3. Visit a bank in your area and observe the processes that are followed. Note down the important attributes of people working in banks.
4. Based on your observation, prepare a report on the important characteristics of a banking operation.
5. Prepare a summary of the differences between the two lists you prepared.

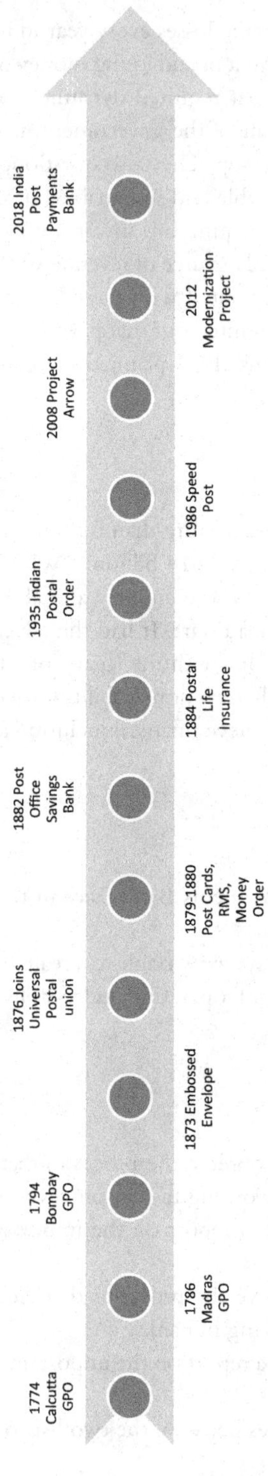

FIGURE 6.1 Important milestones in India Post's journey.

Source: 'Postal History – India Post,' https:www.indiapost.gov.in

TABLE 6.1 India Post Payments Bank: Facilities Provided

- Opening of account through Aadhaar authentication
- Card with QR code with account details
- Interest at 4% per annum for savings accounts
- Zero balance facility
- Deposits up to Rs.1,00,000
- Products:
    - Savings and current accounts
    - Money transfer
    - Direct debit transfers
    - Enterprise and merchant payments
    - Mobile banking
    - Digital banking
    - Doorstep banking

Source: Compiled by the author.

Notes

1 'Prime Minister Launches India Post Payments Bank', *The Hindu*, September 1, 2018.
2 Indiapost.gov.in/VAS/Pages/AboutUs/.
3 upu.int/upu/media/publications/2020-Postal-Development-Report.pdf.
4 Moneycontrol.com/news/business/companies/from-posting-parcels-to-delivery-of-banking-services-will-india-post-succeed-293264.html.
5 Arnab Dutta, 'Is the India Post Payments Bank Financially Sustainable?' Orfonline.org/expert-speak/43671-is-the-india-post-payments-bank-financially-sustainable/.
6 Tamal Bandyopadhyay, 'Can Only Love for Our Postman Ensure Success for India Post Payments Bank', Livemint.com/opinion/. . ./can-only-love-for-our-postman-ensure-success-for-india-post.html.
7 India was under British rule till 1947. When the British left India, the country was partitioned into India and Pakistan, which became separate countries.
8 Arvind Kumar Singh, 'India Post – A Journey through Ages', *National Book Trust*, 2009.
9 A brief history of postal department in India, Rajya Sabha TV, youtube.com/watch?v=MSYFHt4kDwg.
10 Challenges before India Post, www.thehindu.com/opinion/editorial/challenges-before-India-Post/article14938056.ece.
11 Gaurab Dasgupta, 'The Post Truth: Here Is How the Post Office Still Remains Relevant on the Back of Its High-Return Savings Schemes and Accessibility', www.financialexpress.com/money/.
12 Reserve Bank of India had come out with a policy discussion paper on Banking structure in India – The Way Forward, in 2013, which observed that there was a need for niche banking in India. It set up the Nachiket Mor committee to examine the issues relevant to an ubiquitous payments network and universal access to savings.
13 Draft Guidelines for Licensing of 'Payments Banks', www.rbi.org.in/scripts/bs_viewcontent.aspx?Id=2857.
14 Mayank Jain, 'India Post Payments Bank Is Here and Has Problems of Plenty & Legacy', *Business Standard*, September 5, 2018.
15 'India Post Payments Bank Reaches Milestone of 20 Million Customers', *Business Standard*, February 27, 2020.
16 'India Post Payments Bank Customer Base Crosses 50 mn – Mark', *Business Standard*, January 18, 2022.
17 'Cabinet approves Rs.820 Cr financial support to India Posts Payments Bank.'
18 'Post Office Hopes', *Business Standard*, September 6, 2018.
19 'Cabinet Approves Rs.820 Cr Financial Support for India Post Payments Bank', *Business Standard*, April 27, 2022.
20 Indradeep Ghosh and Ajit Ranade, 'Can Payments Banks Succeed?' *Economic & Political Weekly*, *55*(15) (April 11, 2020).

7

PRANA HEALTHCARE

Ujjal Mukherjee, Harold Andrew Patrick, M.H. Sharieff, and Mohammad Salman

Synopsis

Taking a decision regarding the launch of an existing product or product line in a new market is a managerial function. Prana, an Ayurvedic healthcare centre based in Mumbai, was planning to launch a skincare product line in India. Over the years, both the revenue and market size of this family-run business had grown significantly. Besides, the scope and perceived utility of the Ayurveda market as a whole had also grown, and various government-initiated support systems had made Ayurveda a globally recognized practice. Various research and training institutes had been established to support the growth and development of this sector. Ayurvedic hospitals were found across states in India. Dimple Jangda, the founder of Prana, was looking for managerial inputs to help her decide whether or not to launch an Ayurvedic skincare product line.

Introduction

It was 11 p.m. on July 11, 2020. Dimple Jangda (Dimple) took the last sip of her favourite herbal tea before picking up her car keys to drive back home. She could not remember the last time she had enjoyed a leisurely meal with her friends. She had just over two weeks to decide whether to launch 'Prana' branded Ayurvedic[1] skincare products. Dimple, a celebrity Ayurvedic health coach and a gut health[2] expert, had founded Prana, an Ayurvedic healthcare centre in November 2017. Based in Mumbai,[3] Dimple's centre 'Prana' married the 5,000-year-old traditional system of medicine, Ayurveda, with modern research-based science to validate the effectiveness of Ayurvedic methods. Dimple planned to launch an Ayurvedic skincare product line that combined Ayurveda and modern research-based science, moving away from spa-based and inauthentic Ayurvedic products. Her first target market was India, after which she planned to move towards countries like Italy, France, and Spain.

Dimple started Prana as a boot-strapped venture with savings from her investment banking career. The clinic was started as a philanthropic activity to give back to society. The

DOI: 10.4324/9781003261155-12

Prana team of doctors and therapists provided quality healthcare solutions through a holistic approach, combining medicine, ayurvedic diet and treatments, lifestyle changes, personalized diet plans, yoga and fitness, healing, and counselling as and where required. Prana occupied close to 2,900 square feet (nearly 270 square meters) of rented space on the first floor of a residential building in Bandra West,[4] Mumbai. Though it was only around two years old, it already had more than 1,500 regular clients from over 53 countries, including 30+ celebrities from Hollywood and Bollywood. The revenues were increasing every month (an average of US$10,000 per month in the period July to December 2019). During this period, on an average, Prana provided service to 50–70 clients every month.

Prana was doing well in its model of providing healthcare services and Ayurvedic medicines sourced from a reputed supplier in Kerala.[5] However, Dimple's family, friends, and patients, after experiencing the effectiveness of the healthcare services for gut health and chronic diseases, especially skin disorders and customized skincare products provided by Prana, were of the view that she should start an Ayurvedic skincare product line under the 'Prana' banner. These medicines were sent from the Kerala-based manufacturer through a courier service.

The Indian Ayurveda industry was estimated to be worth US$3 billion in 2016, with products accounting for 75% of the market. It was projected to grow by 16% by 2021.[6] On the one hand, Dimple was excited about the growing Ayurvedic medicine market and the 'Make in India'[7] initiative of the Indian government; on the other hand, she was also aware of the existing and growing competition in the market from established Indian skincare brands like Kama Ayurveda, and Forest Essentials, and international brands like The Body Shop.

Moreover, Dimple knew that her team of four employees would not be sufficient to handle the kind of expansion her family was suggesting. The upscaling of 'backward' (additional suppliers, raw materials, etc.) and the addition of 'forward' integration (distributors, retailers, etc.) would require experienced hands. The availability of quality Ayurvedic raw materials and skincare formulations that made these herbs sustainable for shelving and acceptable under USFDA and EU norms had been a perennial challenge for raw material suppliers. Funds were not a big constraint, but the planning had to be robust.

Dimple had a couple of options. Option one was to continue with the current business model of providing customized services and healthcare products and further improve her client base in and around Mumbai. The second option was to continue with the existing business and, additionally, start outsourcing skincare formulations, brand them under the 'Prana' banner, and distribute them in India or overseas. The third option was 'any other possible option.' She had to finalizes her plan by July 30, 2020, failing which she would not be able to book the production capacity of the Kerala-based Ayurvedic medicine manufacturer. This manufacturer commanded a lot of respect in the market because of its ability to manufacture authentic ayurvedic medicines. Importantly, for the first time, the manufacturer was ready to customize a specialized line of skincare formulations for Dimple.

Ayurveda: India and Globe

Ayurveda had a long history and was regarded as one of the oldest healthcare systems in the world. It was a 5,000-year-old Indian holistic healthcare system based on fundamental philosophies about life, disease, and health. Despite the invasion of modern methods of treatment over the millennia, Ayurveda had not only survived in the face of the changing outlook and demands for health services, but had also received acceptance across the globe. Most Indian players in this sector were organized. However, it was difficult to measure the size of the sector because of intra- and inter-sector overlaps. Ayurveda health services included hospitals, clinics, wellness centres, and spas. Ayurveda services involved cross-country mobility of practitioners and patients. The World Health Organization (WHO) had accepted this traditional medicine system. Some of the countries other than India that were influenced by ayurvedic products and services were Pakistan, Bangladesh, Sri Lanka, Maldives, Bhutan, Myanmar, and Nepal. The growing market and its local and global acceptance led the Government of India to form the Ministry of AYUSH (Ayurveda, Yoga & Naturopathy, Unani, Siddha, and Homoeopathy). The All India Institute of Ayurveda (AIIA) was established as an autonomous institute by the Ministry of AYUSH, Government of India. It was a centre of excellence and an apex institute for Ayurveda, aimed at bringing Ayurveda healthcare, training, and education under a single roof. Besides, Ayurveda as a system of medicine had been recognized under the Indian Medicine Central Council (IMCC) Act, 1970. Education was regulated by a statutory body, the Central Council of Indian Medicine (CCIM). The manufacture and sale of Ayurvedic drugs were regulated by the Drugs and Cosmetics Act, 1940. As per the Indian Government's 'Make in India' initiative (launched in September 2014), Ayurveda was a part of the 'wellness' industry. The Ministry of Statistics and Program Implementation (MoSPI)'s National Industrial Classification (NIC) classified Ayurveda as an 'industry.'

The National Health Policy (2017) acknowledged the pluralism in the Indian health sector, wherein traditional and modern medical practices coexisted. The policy focused on mainstreaming the potential of Indian traditional medicine, including Ayurveda. In addition, mainstreaming the potential of AYUSH was one of the priorities of the government. The policy ensured access to AYUSH through the co-location of public facilities. Ayurveda was getting a policy boost in the country, which was likely to further accelerate the growth of the industry.

The market value for herbal cosmetics and skincare items was US$78.5 billion in 2019; from 2020 to 2027, it was estimated to increase at a CAGR of 5.2%. The demand for cosmetics produced without animal testing and without chemical preservatives was increasing and driving the industry's growth. One of the main factors preventing industry growth was a failure to follow worldwide standards. Many natural beauty products were found inadequate when tested according to international standards. One of the reasons for the failure was the low quality of the raw materials used in the production process and the lack of process standardization inside companies which made it difficult for them to adhere to certain laws, especially in the developed markets. The skincare category led the market in 2019 with a 36.6% revenue share. The increase was attributed to a wider understanding of the health advantages of utilizing herbal cosmetics, such as better skin, less acne, and the elimination of fine lines to slow the aging process. The segment was expected to grow with the increase in consumer demand for skincare and hair care products. VLCC, a significant wellness player in South Asia and the Middle East, for instance, had introduced a range of 15 herbal/natural actives-based sun protection products in 2017.

Manufacturing and Distribution of Ayurvedic Products in India

The Ministry of AYUSH had a 'Traditional Knowledge Digital Library' (TKDL). The library had registered around 8.2 million Ayurvedic medical formulations and around 1,150 herbs. According to the Ministry of AYUSH's National Medicinal Plants Board, the Ayurveda,

Siddha, and Unani systems of medicine contained more than 90% plant-based formulations. India had a natural advantage in manufacturing Ayurveda products as over 7,000 indigenous herbal plants were grown in the country. However, there was no up-to-date data on raw material availability. According to official data, the domestic demand for medicinal plants was estimated to be 195,000 metric tons (MT) for the year 2014–2015, and the total consumption of herbal raw drugs in the country was estimated at 512,000 MT. Approximately 22% of the production was sourced through cultivation. According to research, there was a raw material shortage due to an increase in demand for ayurvedic products. For skincare products, the bigger challenge was to source raw materials that were of good quality and not harmful to the skin. Additionally, the products made from such raw materials had to be acceptable to the USFDA[8] and THMPD.[9]

The pilot survey of manufacturers conducted by the Confederation of Indian Industry (CII) showed that many manufacturers had developed well-known Ayurveda brands which were being sold in the domestic as well as international market. The quality of the products was ensured to customers through certificates from reputed agencies such as WHO-GMP (World Health Organization-Good Manufacturing Practices), ISO (International Organization for Standardization) 9000, and HACCAP (Hazard Analysis and Critical Control Points).

Technology had also influenced Ayurveda. E-commerce sales of Ayurvedic products were increasing. The CII survey found that Ayurvedic products and services were reaching out to large segments of the population in a variety of ways due to technological developments. Besides, Ayurvedic products were positioned as medicines, food supplements, or food products. They were sold through Ayurveda-specific pharmacies, general pharmacies, and in-store and non-store (online and social media) retail formats, in both organized and unorganized formats. Manufacturers were positioning their products as Ayurveda, herbal/natural, or organic depending on the market demand. The market demand was growing for all these categories, along with an increase in competition among them.

Prana Healthcare: The Organization

Prana meant 'source of life.' Dimple was known for prescribing ayurvedic diets and principles for daily life. The vision of Prana was to make preventive healthcare science through Ayurveda a global phenomenon and a household practice by simplifying and demystifying the science and bridging the language, cultural, and communication gaps.

Prior to founding Prana, Dimple was a seasoned investment banker and founder of Rudra Investments in New York City. She was also a TV producer at CNBC-TV18, a TV reporter, and a copywriter in advertising. She was on a one-year sabbatical from her career, travelling around the world, trying to find answers to questions she didn't know she had. At one point, she was in Rajasthan and she discovered that she was feeling happy for no reason. The more she thought about it, the more she realized that it was because she was aligned with nature and was in a state of balance. She wanted to bottle this happiness and unconditional bliss and make a viable business of it. Later, she heard about a manufacturer in Kerala whom she wanted to visit. She spent the next few days visiting various ayurvedic manufacturers there. Another four months went into finding a place where she could set up a small ayurvedic clinic in the heart of Mumbai. This was how Prana was born. Ayurveda had helped her to avoid a fifth surgery for herself and surgery for her father's gallbladder and also provided a cure to several issues that close friends and family members had faced. For her, Ayurveda was a way of life, helping to fulfil her desires while caring for her body, mind, and emotions. She understood the food on her plate from the perspective of Doshas,[10] Shadrasa,[11] and Gunas.[12] She planned her workouts, sleeping patterns, and social life based on what her body needed.

The patients at Prana received a personalized Ayurvedic diet chart, medication, and treatment based on their individual prakriti (nature) (see Table 7.1 for the list of diseases/disorders Prana Healthcare helped to prevent and cure).

Ayurvedic Products: Market Research

Both the Indian government and the private sector estimated the size of the Indian Ayurveda industry and the wellness sector. These were largely scattered and one-time estimates of the industry's size and growth potential (see Table 7.2 for the estimates for the Ayurveda and wellness industry as reported by Statistics MRC).

The Dilemma

With just 19 days to go, Dimple needed an answer to whether to continue with the existing business model or launch Prana products in India along with the existing business set-up in

TABLE 7.1 List of Diseases/Issues Cured by Prana

No.	*Major Diseases*	*Subcategories*
1	Chronic pain relief	Joint pain, neck, back, elbow and, frozen shoulder
2	Respiratory disorders	Allergies, asthma and sinusitis
3	Gynaecological disorders	PCOD, infertility and pre, and post-natal therapies
4	Skin diseases	Psoriasis, alopecia, and eczema
5	Psychosomatic disorders	Migraine, anxiety, and insomnia
6	Neurological disorders	Multiple sclerosis and paralysis and facial palsy
7	Eye care	Chronic ailments, glaucoma, computer eye syndrome, and conjunctivitis
8	Musculoskeletal disorders	Cervical and lumbar spondylitis, spondylosis, arthritis, osteoporosis, etc.
9	Lifestyle disorders	Blood pressure, diabetes, obesity, stress and weight management
10	Digestive disorders	Anaemia, piles, acidity, and gastric problems

Source: www.pranabydimple.com/

TABLE 7.2 Size of the Ayurvedic Market

Type of Industry	*Current Size*	*Expected Size*	*Expected Growth Rate*
Global Ayurveda industry	US$3.428 bn as of 2015	US$9.791 by 2022	CAGR 16.2% till 2022
Indian Ayurveda industry	US$3 bn as of 2016	US$4.8 bn by 2021	16% by 2021
Wellness industry	US$13.9 bn as of 2016	US$ more 30 bn by 2021	CAGR 12% by 2021

Source: Report on Ayurveda Industry Market Size, Strength and Way Forward, Confederation Indian Industry (CII), 2018, www.ayurvedaindustry.com/pdf/ayurveda-industry-report.pdf

Mumbai. Or, was there any other viable option? She thought that a consultant might probably be of some help. She knew timing was critical and, therefore, she was looking for actionable recommendations.

Reflective Questions

1. Have you tried any traditional system of medicine for any ailment that you suffered from? What was your experience?
2. Do you think the traditional systems of medicine depend more on trust and are not necessarily based on scientific evidence about their efficacy?
3. Which are the other countries that you are aware of where traditional systems of medicines are popular? What are the reasons for the popularity?

Activities

1. Talk to your friends and relatives and check their awareness of alternative systems of medicine and whether they have tried any of these.
2. Survey the local market in your location and identify the ayurvedic products that are being marketed. Check which of these are from well-known brands and which are from newly introduced brands.

Notes

1 The ancient Indian medical system, also known as Ayurveda, is based on ancient writings that rely on a 'natural' and holistic approach to physical and mental health. Ayurvedic medicine is one of the world's oldest medical systems and remains one of India's traditional healthcare systems. Ayurvedic treatment combines products (mainly derived from plants, but may also include animals, metals, and minerals), diet, exercise, and lifestyle (www.nccih.nih.gov/health/ayurvedic-medicine-in-depth).

2 Gut health describes the function and balance of bacteria of the many parts of the gastrointestinal tract. Ideally, organs such as the esophagus, stomach, and intestines all work together to allow us to eat and digest food without discomfort.

3 Mumbai (formerly called Bombay) is a densely populated city on India's west coast. A financial center, it's India's largest city.

4 Bandra West owes its hip vibe to trendy craft-beer bars and upscale global restaurants, as well as stylish cafes that serve chia juice by day and creative cocktails at night. The area's old-world bungalows sit alongside chic fashion boutiques, wall murals, and street stalls.

5 Kerala, a state on India's tropical Malabar Coast, has nearly 600 km of Arabian Sea shoreline.

6 'Ayurveda Industry – Market Size, Strength and Way Forward', *Confederation of Indian Industry*, 2018.

7 Make in India is an initiative by the Government of India to make and encourage companies to develop, manufacture, and assemble products made in India and to incentivize dedicated investments into manufacturing.

8 The United States Food and Drug Administration (FDA or USFDA) is a federal agency of the Department of Health and Human Services. The FDA is responsible for protecting and promoting public health through the control and supervision of food safety, tobacco products, dietary supplements, prescription, and over-the-counter pharmaceutical drugs (medications), vaccines, biopharmaceuticals, blood transfusions, medical devices, electromagnetic radiation emitting devices (ERED), cosmetics, animal foods and feed, and veterinary products.

9 European Directive on Traditional Herbal Medicinal Products (THMPD). Under this regulation, all herbal medicinal products are required to obtain an authorization to market within the EU.

10 *Dosha* is a central term in Ayurveda originating from Sanskrit, which can be translated into 'that which can cause problems,' and which refers to three categories or types of substances that are

believed to be present in a person's body and mind. A combination of each element results in three humors, or doshas, known as *vata, kapha,* and *pitta.* These doshas are believed to be responsible for a person's physiological, mental, and emotional health.

11 Shadrasa – six tastes. A healthy diet is very important for a healthy body and a healthy mind. An ideal diet, according to Ayurveda, incorporates the six tastes prescribed in the literature and comprises a wide variety of fresh fruits, grains, and milk. Directly and indirectly, these affect the three doshas of an individual. These tastes are sweet, salty, sour, pungent, bitter, and astringent.

12 The gunas explain why one feels lethargic or restless, focused at one time or scattered at another. At any time, only one *guna* can dominate a human being, but for a happy and complete life, it is ideal to strive for a balance in the three gunas. The three gunas are lightness or awareness (*sattva*), activity (*rajas*), and stability or inertia (*tamas*).

Compound annual growth rate (CAGR) is a business and investing specific term for the geometric progression ratio that provides a constant rate of return over the time period.

PART V

Emerging Global Brands

8

READYMADE GARMENT INDUSTRY IN BANGLADESH

Can It Retain the Lead in the Global Market?

Kohinoor Biswas, M. Sayeed Alam, and G.V. Muralidhara

Synopsis

The readymade garment (RMG) industry remained at the heart of Bangladesh's economy since it not only contributed to 84% in the total export earnings in 2020–2021 but also remained as the largest employer in the country employing a workforce of 5 million. Bangladesh had the comparative advantage of cheap labour. In a four-decade long journey, the industry grew from an export value of $31 million to $35.8 billion and was ranked second after China in the global apparel market. The journey was marked by steady growth. However, it was also interrupted by a series of tragic accidents with the deadliest incident claiming more than 1,100 lives in 2013. As a consequence, the RMG industry faced a serious image crisis. Through the collaborative efforts of all the stakeholders, there was significant improvement in workplace safety by 2018.

In 2020, the industry was hit by the COVID-19 global pandemic that caused a loss of $5.6 billion in exports. Within two years, the industry was back on track with the assistance of financial package from the government and the resilience of the workforce. The global market for readymade garments had many supplier countries apart from Bangladesh, namely China, Vietnam, Cambodia, India, Myanmar, and Turkey – Vietnam being the closest competitor. Vietnam enjoyed a number of comparative advantages, like skilled labour, backward linkage, free trade agreement, infrastructure, and FDI, the areas where Bangladesh lagged. It remained to be seen if Bangladesh would be able to transform itself, keep up with the global trends, and maintain its position in the global RMG market.

Introduction

Bangladesh celebrated 50 years of its independence in 2021. A country with a GDP of less than $7 billion in 1972, Bangladesh had achieved a GDP of $416 billion by 2021 and is aspiring to become a middle-income country by 2031. In this journey, one industry that played

DOI: 10.4324/9781003261155-14

a key role was the RMG industry. RMG contributed 84% of the total exports of Bangladesh in the period July– 2020–June 2021 and the country was ranked second after China in global apparel exports.[1]

July 28, 1978, was the day when independent Bangladesh started exporting RMG. The earliest consignment consisting of 10,000 pieces of shirts was exported to France by Reaz Garments Limited founded by Mohammad Reazuddin (Reazuddin).[2] Reazuddin received appreciation from Neil Armstrong, Michael Collins, and Edwin Aldrin, the Apollo-11 astronauts when they visited Dhaka as part of their World Goodwill Tour on October 27, 1969. By 2021, the RMG industry witnessed steady growth and achieved a 1,000-point jump in total export value from as low as $31 million in 1983–1984 to $35.8 billion in 2020–2021.[3]

During the period 1974–2004, the RMG in the developing countries enjoyed quota facilities under the provision of Multi-Fiber Arrangement (MFA). During this period, the government of Bangladesh took proactive measures that helped in the steady growth of the industry. This was followed by a 'no-quota' phase once the MFA ended in 2004. During this phase, the industry kept up with innovation, product diversification, automation, skill, and capacity-building. From 2005 to 2019, the industry exports grew from $10.52 to $16.88 billion, registering an overall growth of 60%.

The global pandemic COVID-19 hit in March 2020 and posed a new round of challenges. The industry dwindled temporarily, yet bounced back in about two years.[4,5]

Bangladesh reached the second position globally, replacing Vietnam in 2021, China being the market leader in the RMG market. Though the Bangladesh RMG industry had managed a well-crafted growth in the past, there was no guarantee that the trend would continue in the future. Vietnam enjoyed comparative advantages over Bangladesh on a number of areas: value-added product, foreign direct investment (FDI), diversification, backward linkage, human skills, and preferential agreement with EU.[6] Given the tough competition, can Bangladesh retain the lead in the global RMG market?

Bangladesh

The People's Republic of Bangladesh (Bangladesh) earned freedom from Pakistan on December 16, 1971, after a nine-month long blood-showered civil war at the cost of 3 million lives. It was one of the most densely populated countries in the world. Endowed with natural beauty, portrayed in blue, with the Bay of Bengal on the south-eastern side, it had the longest sea beach in the world – Cox's Bazar. On the south-western side, it was portrayed in green, with the Sundarbans, the largest mangrove forest of the world.[7,8]

Bangladesh RMG

Reaz Garments, Desh Garments, Bond Garments, Paris Garments, Azim Group, and Sunman Group were among the early entrants in the Bangladesh RMG industry during the late 1970s. In 1978, Reaz garments exported 1 million pieces of shirts to South Korea. Though there was an increase in export value yet, Bangladesh RMG could not diversify either its product basket or its export market destination (see Table 8.1). The industry was not keeping abreast of the global market trend (see Table 8.2) as well. There were only nine export-oriented garment factories in 1978.[9]

TABLE 8.1 Bangladesh RMG Lacking Product and Market Diversification

	Export Basket of Bangladesh RMG	*Export Market Destination of Bangladesh RMG*
1993–1994	Shirts, T-shirts, jacket, trouser and sweater: comprised 79.6% of total export	EU and the United States comprised 78% of export
2018–2019	Shirts, T-shirts, jacket, trouser, and sweater: comprised 73% of total export	EU and the United States comprised 83.4% of export

Source: www.mckinsey.com/industries/retail/our-insights/whats-next-for-bangladeshs-garment-industry-after-a-decade-of-growth

TABLE 8.2 Global Trend: Cotton-based Apparel versus Man-made Fiber-based Apparel

	Bangladesh	*Global (between 2007 and 2017)*
Cotton-based apparel	Share was 68% in 2008–2009 and increased to 74.14% in 2020	Global share was 35%, shrinking at 0.5% only
Man-made fibre apparel (MMF)	Share was only 5% in the global MMF trade	Global share was 45%, growing at 5%

Source: www.businesswire.com/news/home/20191025005178/en/Global-1182.9-Billion-Clothing-Apparel-Market-Analysis

M. Shamsur Rahman of Stylecraft Limited, the first President of Bangladesh Garment Manufacturers and Exporters Association (BGMEA) and AM Subid Ali of Aristocrat Limited, contributed to the growth of the industry in the initial years. A group of energetic and enthusiastic entrepreneurs joined the industry and continued in their footsteps. In 1983, BGMEA was established to encourage and maintain the interest of RMG manufacturers and exporters in Bangladesh. This organization was initiated with the aim of collaborating with local and international brands, development partners, and stakeholders. Since then, there was no looking back. In 1983–1984, the total export from RMG was valued at $31.5 million, contributing just 3.9% of the total exports from Bangladesh. With an impressive growth, by 2020–2021 the industry achieved a total of $35.8 billion worth of exports, contributing 84% of the total exports and around 12% of GDP of Bangladesh. BGMEA had a total of 5,500 member factories in 2021, employing 5 million people, of which 85% were rural women.[10]

Overview of Global RMG

The size of global RMG was valued at $983.7 billion in 2019 and was expected to grow at a compounded annual growth rate (CAGR) of 8.8%, reaching $1,268.3 billion by 2027. China, the global market leader, posted a total export value of $115 billion; Bangladesh, the second with $35.8 billion; Vietnam, the third, with $31 billion. India with 16.9 billion and Turkey with 15.5 billion in 2019 were the other major players.[11]

It was projected that between 2020 and 2025, Asia-Pacific, Africa, Middle East, and South America would continue to grow at a CAGR of 15.4%, 14.3% 14.0%, and 11.6%, respectively.[12]

The Allied Market Research, a subsidiary of Allied Analytics, a US-based global market research and consulting firm published a report in April 2022. It reported that the global

TABLE 8.3 Projected Growth in the Global RMG Industry in 2021–2027

Category	*Projected Compounded Annual Growth Rate (CAGR) in 2021–2027 in the Global Market*
Formal wear	9.1%
Outer clothing	8.8%
Woven segment	9.1%
Adult segment	9.1%
Kids segment	9.4%

Source: https://textilefocus.com/global-readymade-garments-market-size-projected-reach-1268–3-billion-2027-new-research-says/

RMG market was fragmented with 8.07% occupied by the major players such as Louis Vuitton, NIKE, Adidas AG, VF Corporation, Hanesbrands Inc., GAP, H&M, Zara, Under Armour, PVH Corporation, and Benetton Group.[13] The report also projected a good growth in the period 2021–2027 in the global apparel market (see Table 8.3).

Growth during the MFA Era (1974–2004)

Multi-Fiber Arrangement (MFA) was introduced in 1974 by the World Trade Organization (WTO) with the objective of patronizing developing nations with comparative advantage of low labour cost. Under its provision 40 nations, including Bangladesh, were provided quota or duty-free access to the developed market. Initially, MFA was made effective till 1994 that was subsequently changed to the Agreement on Textiles and Clothing (ATC), which expired on January 1, 2005.[14]

In the early 1980s, the Bangladesh government issued licenses to import duty-free garment machinery to manufacture export products. As a result, the number of garment factories in Bangladesh increased rapidly from 47 in 1982 to 632 in 1984–1985 and 2,900 in 1999. The industry grew roughly at an average rate of 22% during the 1990s.[15] In the 1980s, government offered bonded warehouse facilities for 100% export-oriented garment factories, enabling them to easily import the essential fabrics and accessories. The competitiveness of the RMG industry was further enhanced by reducing production delay and bureaucracy. The first Export Processing Zone (EPZ) was established in 1983, which offered foreign investors a ten-year tax holiday, duty-free import of machinery and raw materials, bonded warehouses, and initiatives such as back-to-back Letter of Credit (LC).[16] The BGMEA University of Fashion and Technology was established in 2012, offering graduate and postgraduate degrees in fashion design, knitwear technology, and apparel merchandising with the aim of building appropriate skill sets for the industry.[17]

Post- MFA Era: Overcoming Challenges

There was anticipation with tension from all quarters that expiry of MFA would hurt the industry. However, Bangladesh proved it otherwise through various proactive measures. In 2005–2006, the very first year after the phasing out of MFA, the industry posted a total export value of $7.9 billion, which was $1.48 billion more than the previous year, registering a 23.11% growth. This achievement was attributed to various factors that included continuous support from the government, low wage rate, large-scale production capacity, and competitive price- accompanied by a stable exchange rate and political stability since 2007. The report published in 2015 by the World Bank's Diagnostic Trade Integration Study endorsed these findings.

Accidents in Bangladesh RMG: Aftermath and Turnaround

There were a series of scattered accidents in different garment factories (see Table 8.4) in Bangladesh since 2005, with the worst one in 2013 claiming more than 1,100 lives.[18] Poor compliances, sub-standard working environment, extensive sub-contracting, and lower prices offered by the international retailers were cited as the main reasons for the frequent tragic incidents. As a reaction to these incidents, some international buyers cancelled orders. The United States withdrew the duty-free access to some selected items in response to the deadliest accident in 2013.[19]

In the aftermath of the accidents the industry took the issue of image crisis seriously. The Accord on Fire and Building Safety was signed on May 15, 2013. It was a five-year independent, legally binding agreement among the global brands; retailers and trade unions intended to build a safe and healthy RMG in Bangladesh. The Accord focused on issues like independent inspection, transparent Corrective Action Plans (CAP), democratically elected safety committees and worker empowerment through awareness (see Table 8.5).[20] Another body was established in the same year, namely the Alliance for Bangladesh Worker Safety with a tenure of five years. In 2018, as the term of the five-year agreement ended, the Alliance achieved a number of milestones on providing safety training, ensuring transparency on reporting and creating a 24-hour confidential worker helpline (see Table 8.6).[21]

The RMG Sustainability Council (RSC) was established on June 1, 2020, to take forward the work of the local Bangladesh Accord and Alliance office. The RSC represented three parties: apparel industry, global fashion brands, and local trade unions. Alongside, BGMEA tightened membership criterion in order to ensure safety. Workers became more aware of

TABLE 8.4 Death Toll in the Bangladesh RMG at a Glance

Year	*Incident*	*Death Toll*	*Injury*
January 2005	Fire accident in a garment factory	22	
April 2005	Building collapsed	64	100
February 2006	Building collapsed	21	Few dozens
February 2006	Fire accident in a textile factory	65	Few dozens
February 2010	Fire accident in a garment factory	21	50
December 2010	Fire accident in a garment factory	26	100
November 2012	Fire accident in a garment factory	112	150
April 2013	Building collapsed	1,136	Few hundreds
2014	Boiler burst	1	4
2014	Fire accident in a garment factory	0	3
2015	Fire accident in a garment factory	0	38
2016	Boiler burst	34	70

Source: www.reuters.com/article/us-bangladesh-blast-accidents-factbox-idUSKBN19P0JN

TABLE 8.5 Six Key Components of the Accord on Fire and Building Safety in Bangladesh

1. An agreement with five-year long legal binding between brands and trade unions to safeguard a safe working environment in the Bangladeshi RMG industry
2. A self-governing inspection programme supported by brands in which workers and trade unions are engaged
3. Full disclosure of all inspection reports and corrective action plans (CAP) made public
4. A pledge by signatory brands to confirm sufficient funds availability for remediation and maintaining relationships with sourcing partners
5. To ensure a democratic process in electing members in the health and safety committees in all factories to identify and act on health and safety risks
6. Worker awareness and empowerment through an extensive training programme, anonymous complaints mechanism and right to refuse unsafe work

Source: www.business-humanrights.org/en/latest-news/the-accord-on-fire-and-building-safety-in-bangladesh/

their safety. Forming a safety committee became a prerequisite in the garment factories across the country according to the compliance requirements.[22]

Subcontracting to non-compliant factories was one of the sources of accidents. In 2019, the government issued a strict guideline that limited subcontracting only to the compliant factories. Yet there remained tension between government and the garment workers. There were several cases of protests by the garment workers alleging unfair wages.

Set Back due to COVID-19

The global pandemic COVID-19 hit on March 2020, as a result of which the RMG industry in Bangladesh was affected badly on multiple fronts. Many of the airports and seaports were locked down globally, which disrupted not only the sourcing of raw materials from China but also shipping the final products from Bangladesh to the EU and US market. There were cancellation of new orders. Overall, the RMG industry was at a peril.[23] A total number of 232 RMG factories were closed down and a total number of 357,000 employees lost their jobs during this time period. Consequently, Bangladesh RMG experienced 16.9% decline in export earnings in 2020 compared to 2019, registering a net loss of $5.6 billion.[24]

Resurgence of the Industry Post-COVID

Bangladesh government provided salary stimulus package and interest-free loans to the garment owners for paying wages and benefits to workers during the COVID-19 pandemic. After five months into the pandemic in August 2020, the situation started rebounding with export value posted at $3.24 billion.[25]

Vietnam: A Tough Contender to Bangladesh

During the period 2015–2019, Bangladesh was ranked second and Vietnam third in the global RMG market. In 2020–2021, during COVID-19 regime Vietnam overtook Bangladesh, taking the second position. However, Bangladesh regained its runner-up position in 2021.[26] Vietnam struck some free trade agreements with countries in promising markets.

TABLE 8.6 Highlights from Alliance Fifth Annual Report 2018

- 93% of improvement across Alliance-affiliated factories is complete, including 90% of risky items
- 428 factories have finalized all necessary items in their initial Corrective Action Plans (CAPs)
- Nearly 1.6 million workers have been trained to protect themselves in case of a fire emergency
- 28,000 security guards received training in fire safety and emergency evacuation procedures
- More than 1.3 million workers across 941 Alliance and non-Alliance factories have access to *Amader Kotha*, the Alliance's confidential worker Helpline
- More than 1.5 million workers now have access to a 24-hour confidential worker helpline, which has been relocated to local management under Phulki and will soon be available to RMG factories throughout Bangladesh
- 181 worker safety committees have been made, giving workers a seat at the table with management in resolving safety issues

Source: www.bangladeshworkersafety.org/488-2018-annual-report-press-release

TABLE 8.7 Country-wise Competitiveness Assessment in the Global RMG Market

	Production Quality	*Ability to Create Value-added Product*	*Ability to Source Raw materials*	*Innovation*	*Efficiency*	*Lead Time*	*Political Stability*	*Sustainability*
Bangladesh	3.5	3	2	3	3	3.5	2.5	2
Cambodia	3.5	3	2	2	3	3	3.5	2.5
Laos	3.5	2.5	2.5	2.5	2	2	3	2
Nepal	2	2	3	2.5	3	2	3	2
China	4.5	4.5	5	4.5	4.5	4	2.5	2
Vietnam	4.5	4	3	4	4	4.5	4.5	3.5

Source: www.tbsnews.net/economy/rmg/bangladesh-apparel-less-competitive-vietnams-360952

Industry experts attributed Vietnam's success to a number of factors, like skilled workforce, diversified and value-added products, and Foreign Direct Investment (FDI).[27]

Asian Productivity Organization (APO) reported in 2020 that the per-worker annual productivity level in Bangladesh garment industry was $10,400 against $12,600 in Vietnam. Industry experts attributed the low productivity in Bangladesh to lack of training, a proper work environment, and poor investment in education. In Vietnam, 5% of GDP was invested in education, while in Bangladesh it was only 2% in 2019–2020. Vietnam also demonstrated a clear edge over Bangladesh in product diversification. About 79% export from Vietnam counted for ten varieties of product, whereas 73% from Bangladesh came from only five products. For every 100 kg of t-shirts, Vietnam earned $2,160 compared to Bangladesh, which earned $1,100.

RMG industry in Vietnam started its journey in 1986. Structural reforms led by state-owned enterprises (SOEs) resulted in technological improvement, enhanced managerial capability, and product diversification. Vietnam established spinning and textile industry that supplied around 60% of fabric and accessories, which became possible due to proximity to China.[28] On the other hand, RMG in Bangladesh remained very weak in backward linkage serving just 5–8% of total demand, forcing the industry to remain import-dependent. As a result, 60–70% of the realization went for imports[29] (see Table 8.7). Vietnam enjoyed

TABLE 8.8 Garments Manufacturing Labour Costs (US$/hour) by Countries

Asian Competitors	*Labour Cost $ per Hour*
Bangladesh	0.22 (72% cheaper than Vietnam)
Cambodia	0.33
Pakistan	0.37
Vietnam	0.38
Sri Lanka	0.43
Indonesia	0.44
India	0.51
China (remote/inland areas)	0.55–0.80
China (other coastal/core areas)	0.86–0.94
China (prime coastal areas)	1.08
Malaysia	1.18
Thailand	1.29–1.36

Source: www.onlineclothingstudy.com/2013/07/labour-cost-us-hour-in-readymade.html

lead time of 30 days to the EU market, which was about 90 days for Bangladesh. However, Bangladesh had an advantage over other competing countries in terms of its labour cost (see Table 8.8).

Competitive Pressure from Other Suppliers in the Global RMG

India, Turkey, and Cambodia were ranked fourth, sixth, and ninth, respectively, in the global RMG market in 2019. India had better labour productivity per hour with $6.4 against $3.45 for Bangladesh. India, being the largest cotton producer enjoyed a clear cost advantage in cotton-based apparel. Turkey had enjoyed not only location advantage due to proximity to EU market but also quota facility to EU market. Though Bangladesh was ahead of Cambodia on competitiveness (see Table 8.7) and Cambodia entered in RMG market 12 years later than Bangladesh, the country was eyeing economic growth relying on this sector. By ensuring higher standard of workers' rights and workplace safety, Cambodia accessed the US market.[30] Ethiopia, a country with only $145 million of RMG export in 2021, came into the scenario as a competitor mainly on its strength of cheapest labour and free trade agreements with the United States and EU[31] (see Table 8.9).

Challenges and Road Ahead

Industry experts emphasized that cheap labour that worked so far as a comparative advantage for Bangladesh would not be sustainable in future. Vietnam attracted buyers because of its ability to produce high-end products. Furthermore, enhancing the skill level of workers was important.

Creating a favourable country image in the global marketplace was another top agenda prescribed by the industry insiders. Bangladesh had suffered from a serious image crisis as a consequence of fatal accidents in the garment factories in 2012–2013. Though government intervention improved workplace safety, thereby reducing number of accidents significantly, still the government would need to remain vigilant in order to prevent the repetition of

TABLE 8.9 Ethiopia Report Card, 2019

Export earnings in 2021	$145 million
Vision 2030 for RMG	$30 billion
Doing Business rank	159 (nine place ahead of Bangladesh)
Labour cost	$26 a month, which is 3.65 times less than that of Bangladesh ($95 a month)
FDI	USA (US brands: H&M, Gap, and PVH), China
Partnering with China	Flagship Hawassa Industrial Park by the Chinese
Duty-free access to USA and EU	For 20% cotton-based product and 30% for non-cotton-based product

Source: https://rmgbd.net/2019/05/ethiopias-garment-workers-are-worlds-lowest-paid/; https://thefinancialexpress.com.bd/special-issues/rmg-textile-4/ethiopia-a-new-competitor-for-bangladesh-rmg-export-1509290838

such incidents. Experts also blamed the weak road, port, and technological infrastructure of Bangladesh for poor competitiveness of its RMG.

Reflective Questions

1. How can Bangladesh RMG overcome the competitive pressure from Vietnam when Vietnam is enjoying preferential agreement with EU and was way ahead in FDI than Bangladesh? What steps should the industry take to combat other competitors, such as Cambodia, India, and Turkey?
2. How can Bangladesh RMG race against competitors with low-cost edge with African nations like Ethiopia offering better cost advantage to the global buyers? What should be the strategies for the industry to craft in order to divert from cost pressure from the global buyers?
3. How can Bangladesh RMG handle the challenge of maintaining workplace safety and remaining profitable at the same time?

Suggested Activities

Form teams of three or four students and complete the following activities.

1. Suggest a roadmap for the Bangladesh RMG to keep abreast of global trends.
2. Conduct a SWOT analysis for Bangladesh RMG industry.
3. Prepare a plan to enhance the skill level of workers in the Bangladesh RMG industry.

Notes

1 www.mckinsey.com/industries/retail/our-insights/whats-next-for-bangladeshs-garment-industry-after-a-decade-of-growth.
2 www.tbsnews.net/feature/panorama/reazuddin-tailor-who-became-first-rmg-exporter-bangladesh-196057.
3 www.bgmea.com.bd/page/Export_Performance.
4 https://thefinancialexpress.com.bd/views/views/your-order-has-been-cancelled-the-coronavirus-impact-on-the-rmg-sector-1584974682.
5 www.orfonline.org/research/bangladesh-covid19-badly-impacts-garments-industry-65275/.

6 www.businesswire.com/news/home/20191025005178/en/Global-1182.9-Billion-Clothing-Apparel-Market-Analysis.
7 www.bangladesh.com/travel/geography/.
8 https://bangladeshembassy.ru/about-bangladesh/basic-facts-about-bangladesh/.
9 https://businessinspection.com.bd/rmg-industry-of-bangladesh/.
10 www.bgmea.com.bd/page/AboutGarmentsIndustry.
11 https://rmgbd.net/2022/04/the-global-readymade-garments-market-size-is-projected-to-reach-1268-3-billion-by-2027-new-research-says/.
12 https://shenglufashion.com/2021/12/27/statistics-global-apparel-market-2021-2026/.
13 https://textilefocus.com/global-readymade-garments-market-size-projected-reach-1268–3-billion-2027-new-research-says/.
14 https://againstthecurrent.org/atc125/p185/.
15 www.mckinsey.com/industries/retail/our-insights/whats-next-for-bangladeshs-garment-industry-after-a-decade-of-growth.
16 www.thedailystar.net/news-detail-229891.
17 https://archive.dhakatribune.com/business/real-estate/2020/02/24/bangladesh-rmg-timeline.
18 www.thedailystar.net/1-841-workers-killed-in-12-yrs-19973.
19 www.tbsnews.net/feature/panorama/six-ways-bangladeshs-rmg-industry-changed-after-rana-plaza-collapse-236395.
20 https://bangladeshaccord.org/.
21 www.bangladeshworkersafety.org/.
22 www.rsc-bd.org/en.
23 https://orfonline.org/research/bangladesh-covid19-badly-impacts-garments-industry-65275/.
24 https://pedl.cepr.org/publications/economic-effects-covid-19-ready-made-garment-factories-bangladesh.
25 www.policyforum.net/bangladeshs-road-to-recovery.
26 https://businessinspection.com.bd/rmg-landscape-vietnam-vs-bangladesh/.
27 www.thedailystar.net/opinion/news/bangladesh-rmg-time-look-beyond-the-comparative-advantage-cheap-labour-1985885.
28 www.fibre2fashion.com/industry-article/8705/evolution-of-vietnam-s-textiles-garments-industry-amid-covid-19.
29 www.textileblog.com/backward-linkages-in-the-textile-industry/.
30 www.lightcastlebd.com/insights/2020/08/the-fashion-war-that-matters-assessing-bangladesh-rmgs-international-competitiveness/.
31 https://rmgbd.net/2019/05/ethiopias-garment-workers-are-worlds-lowest-paid/.

PART VI

Digital Transformation

9

JUPITER

A Neobank Revolution in the Indian Banking System

Bhagyashree Narayan and D.B. Bharati

Synopsis

This case is about the neobank 'Jupiter,' a Mumbai-based FinTech startup that was in the limelight for its digital-only core banking products and gained attention for attracting funds from global investors. Jupiter was the fastest growing startup in India in the neobank space with services offered through the invite-only way for customer onboarding. Jupiter had raised a total of $157 million in funding series round, and by December 2021 it was valued at US$711 million. The company wanted to 'deliver a personalized banking experience with the mindset of an internet company.'

The case highlights Jupiter neobank's FinTech-based business model which was proposed with interchange margins and digital services to value customers with no hidden fees. Though Jupiter raised huge funds, still it was in need of US$200–300 million over the next five years. The crowded conventional banking system and new digital banks market created competition and challenges for sustainability. The case discusses the business model of Jupiter, its fundraising pattern and valuation basis, and business opportunities and challenges.

Keywords: FinTech, neobank, fundraising and valuation basis, business model, challenges.

> We wanted to deliver a personalized banking experience with the mindset of an internet company. Our customer service is not differentiated based on a customer's balance, and we give them an instant resolution to their needs.[1]
>
> *CA Jitendra Gupta, Jupiter founder & CEO, in September 2021*

DOI: 10.4324/9781003261155-16

Introduction

On December 27, 2021, India-based neobank[2] Jupiter raised US$86 million in new funding round, Series C, led by QED Investors,[3] and Sequoia growth fund.[4] After this round of fundraising, the valuation of the company stood at US$711 million and total funds raised were at US$155 million as of December 2021. Jupiter was founded by Jitendra Gupta[5] (Gupta) in the year 2019. The founder leveraged his finance and banking experience and introduced the Jupiter neobank in the FinTech space. Jupiter initiated its offerings of basic banking products like digital savings bank and payment gateway through its beta version in June 2021; the launch of beta version witnessed more than 0.15 million requests from users for early access within the first two weeks of launch. The bank opened the digital platform to users through the invite-only model. The company claimed that more than 3,000 customers joined the platform and that it had attracted over $1 million deposits within a month of launch.

Jupiter partnered with Federal Bank[6] and Visa[7] to issue Zero balance savings accounts and debit cards. It powered the core banking solutions to digitally savvy customers as an internet company without any physical branches The bank offered innovative financial products and services like Pots, Rewards, Insights (refer to Table 9.1); with security it had created a huge impact on the mindsets of the new customers.

The Fintech Market in India

The Indian FinTech market had witnessed an exponential rise in funding after 2016. The total funding in FinTech space from 2016 to 2021 stood at $16.5 billion, of which around 60% was after 2019. However, India remained an untapped market due to the low penetration of financial services with about 14.6% of the Indian population remaining unbanked. The Indian market witnessed incredible growth in digital payments, with transaction volume reaching $2 trillion approximately in September 2021 from $1.30 trillion in September 2020. According to a report by BLinC Insights,[8] the overall size of the financial service sector in India was estimated at US$500 billion, of which the FinTech market accounted for $31 billion in 2021. Preferred FinTech segments consisted of Investment tech, Lending, Payments,

TABLE 9.1 Products and Services Offered by Jupiter

Pots	*Insights*	*Rewards*
• A space in Jupiter account was designed to help customers to save for specific goals like travel funds, phone upgrades, any purchase, etc. • It was away from the main balance • Possible to create multiple Pots • Add and withdraw money anytime • Earn interest on the Pots balances	• Insights help to get real-time spending breakdowns with smart categorizations like health, rent, bills, etc. • Quick and easy views of money moves • Spend details with notification	• A cashback value calculated on the net purchase transaction value depending on the offer applicability, offer instruction, and terms and conditions supplemented on a time-to-time basis

Source: https://life.jupiter.money

Banking Infra, and others. The central government initiative of Digital India[9] had created a favourable growth potential for Indian FinTech. The landscape of neobanking in India was expected to become mainstream with more customers and small companies opting for neobanks for their banking needs. According to Dataquest,[10] the global neobanking market stood $47.39 billion in 2021 and was projected to grow at CAGR of 53.4% between 2021 and 2030.

India is the second most populous country after China, with a population of about 1.31 billion as of 2021, which is roughly one-sixth of the world's total population. Millennials accounted for about 34% of the total population in India. According to a joint publication report by NASSCOM[11] and KPMG,[12] rising customer expectations, e-commerce, and smartphone penetration have played a massive role in driving FinTech in India.

Jupiter

Jupiter was the second venture founded by FinTech veteran Gupta, who had earlier co-founded payment platform company Citrus Pay. He sold Citrus Pay for US$130 million in 2016 to PayU. Gupta was Managing Director at PayU India and launched buy-now-pay-later (BNPL)[13] products in the country. Gupta gauged that the Indian customers were not happy with the existing banks, their processes, experiences, mindsets, and behaviour of the staff. Gupta sensed that customers were looking for a service that was simpler, quicker, and wanted a different approach. Then he founded the neobank platform Jupiter, owned and operated by Amica Financial Technology Private Limited in 2019.[14] Jupiter provided a digital banking platform where users could open a zero-balance bank account digitally and get a visa debit card. The users also got insight into spending on a real-time basis. The other services offered by Jupiter were a pro-salary account with no hidden fees, and various rewards. Additionally, reading resources – a collection of life hacks to improve financial wellness, a Portfolio analyser,[15] and various calculators for customers' were offered by Jupiter. The company earned revenue from interchange fees levied on customers when they swipe their debit or credit cards, transfers, and payments. Jupiter exercised extensive social connections through various platforms to interact with customers, update them about products. It also highlighted the ease of doing banking with them.

Expedition of Jupiter

The startup partnered with Federal Bank and Axis Bank for banking business. Jupiter had raised US$25 million as seed funding (refer to Table 9.2) US$2 million in the Series A round within four months of incorporation. The company acquired Easyplan backed by Y Combinator, an AI-powered[16] financial saving application that had over 0.25 million users. In August 2021, the company had raised US$44 million in a Series B funding round where it was valued at US$290 million. In December 2021, it raised US$86 million as a part of its Series C funding round co-led by Tiger Global Management, Sequoia Capital India, after which its valuation increased to $711 million (refer to Table 9.3). The company planned to use these funds for technological advancements and for the development of lending products. It aimed to onboard 2 million customers by December 2022;

Jupiter began inviting customers to join the waitlist before taking its core banking platform live. It relied on the invite-only business model to generate user interest; it came out

TABLE 9.2 Jupiter: Fundraising Rounds

Announced Date	*Transaction Type*	*Number of Investors*	*Money Raised*	*Lead Investors*
December 27, 2021	Series C – Jupiter	10	$86 million	QED Investors, Sequoia Capital India, Tiger Global Management
August 5, 2021	Series B – Jupiter	11	$45 million	Global Founders Capital, Matrix Partners India, Nubank, Sequoia Capital India
April 8, 2020	Series A – Jupiter	2	$2 million	Hummingbird Ventures, Bedrock Capital
November 5, 2019	Seed Round – Jupiter	7	$25 million	Sequoia Capital India

Source: www.crunchbase.com/organization/amica-financial-technologies/investor_financials

TABLE 9.3 FinTech Startup: Funding and Valuation

Evolution Stages	*Sources of Capital*	*Funding Size*	*Valuation Range (Approx.)*	*Basis*
Idea only	Seed funds/ angel investor/ personal/friends and family	$50,000–100,000	$500,000– 1.5 million	The attractiveness of the idea and its market size
Team-building	Seed funds/angel/ personal/friends and family	$100,000–250,000	$500,000– 1.5 million	Founders, teammates, and their capacity to execute
Prototype	Seed funds/angel investor	$250,000–500,000	$2–5 million	A successful working model of service/product
Minimum Viable Product (MVP)	Seed funds/angel investor/VCs	$1–5 million	$5–20 million	Customer adoption and cashflow in the business
Rapid customer adoption	Series A angels, seed funds exit, VCs increase	$5–20 million	>$50 million	Strong estimates on growth, market share, revenue
Viral growth capital for long term	Multiple rounds series B, C, D, E The partial exit of VCs Entry of PE	$20–100 million	>$250 million	Growth as estimated, exceeding revenue, profitability
Stability	Steady growth	>$100 million	>$500 million	Cash flow and profitability

Source: Adapted from an online article by Nirvikar Jain, Finance Expert. www.toptal.com/finance/valuation/how-to-value-a-fintech-startup

with the 'Mission-Invite' programme to let existing users invite their connections. Customers without an invite can download the Jupiter application to get limited invites from the maker of the app. Jupiter planned to cater to the under-tapped segment of society specifically, the retail customers, MSME enterprises, in tier-I and tier-II cities, rural areas, and digital millennials who received limited attention in the existing banking systems. According to Gupta, 'Neobank space did not follow an established path hence turned out to be whitespace.'[17,18]

Competition

Jupiter dived into the highly competitive banking industry wherein traditional banks and digital banks struggled to exist. Praxis Global Alliance[19] consultants said, 'Traditional banks are trapped in archaic and more costly ways of working, while brick-and-mortar lenders have mobile apps and online banking, they are not purely digital and customers still need to visit branches for certain processes.'[20] According to Gupta, Jupiter does not consider the traditional banks as their competitors, and for him competition was mainly from the digital-only banks. The digital banks majorly offered products and services on technology platforms that were also used by Jupiter. In the Neobank category, there were 16 FinTech companies in India as of December 2021. The top neobank competitors included Fi, Niyo, and InstaPay (refer to Table 9.4).

Challenges and Future

As per the central advisory study, 'neobanks are cheaper and much more flexible, and agile than traditional banks.'[21] However, building trust and relationships has been a major challenge for these banks. The existing regulations in India did not allow digital banks to obtain bank

TABLE 9.4 Top Players in Indian Neobanking Industry

	Jupiter	*Fi*	*Niyo*	*InstantPay*
CEO	Jitendra Gupta	Sujith Narayanan	Vinay Bagri	Shailendra Agarwal
Establishment	2019	2019	2015	2013
No. of employees	300	135	500	90
Seed round	$25 million		$1 million	$5.07 million
Series A funding	$2 million	$13 million	$13.2 million	–
Series B funding	$44 million	$50 million	$35 million	–
Series C funding	$86 million	–	$100 million	–
Funding from existing investors	–	$12 million	–	–
Total Funding	$157 million	$75 million	$149.2 million	$5.07 million
Operating revenue in FY21	0.018 million	0	243 million	350 million
Users as of December 2021	0.5 million	1M	4 million	10 million

Source: www.cbinsights.com/research/niyo-competitors-walrus-fi-jupiter

licenses and they needed to partner with traditional banks for providing licensed services. Gupta explained:

> To build a large sustainable and prosperous neobank in India, you will need at least $200–300 million over the next five years. And it is only because the initial investment in infrastructure is very high. The money that goes into security compliances, the liquidity ratios you need to maintain, the investment in customer service, etc. is huge. We now know why the banks are slow to act. Our challenge is therefore to maintain the fine balance between compliance and agility.[22]

He also said, 'Jupiter would not be going for too many partnerships as they want customers to come to their proposition and not only business.'[23]

Reflective Questions

1. Critically analyse the business model of Jupiter.
2. Examine fundraising pattern and valuation of Jupiter.
3. Discuss the challenges faced by Jupiter in domestic Neobanking. How should Jupiter manage the show?

Learning Activities

Study the banking ecosystem in your country. Identify the new-age players who focus on providing a totally digital banking service. Compare these with the traditional brick and mortar banks in terms of the infrastructure, manpower, revenue models, customer acquisition, and customer experience.

Notes

1 Anwesha Singha, 'How Jitendra Gupta-led Jupiter Is Building Its Neobanking Space', https://indianstartupnews.com, April 27, 2022.
2 NeoBank refers to digital bank which does not have any physical branches.
3 The US-based premier venture capital firm that supports high-growth companies and businesses.
4 Venture capital fund managed by Sequoia Capital. The fund is based in Menlo Park, California, and invests around the globe. The fund mainly invests in the technology sector.
5 Commerce graduate and Qualified Chartered Accountant, Jitendra Gupta worked with ICICI Bank for seven years in the investment banking division. He was the founder of Citrus Pay and Lazypay and was also the MD of PayU India.
6 An Indian private sector bank headquartered in Kochi, India. The bank has 1,272 branches spread across different states in India.
7 American multinational financial services company which facilitates electronic fund transfer throughout the world, most commonly VISA branded credit cards, debit cards, and prepaid cards.
8 India-based venture capital fund.
9 Digital India is a flagship programme of the Government of India with a vision to transform India into a digitally empowered society and knowledge economy; launched in July 2015.
10 An Indian magazine focused on information technology–related articles.
11 National Association of Software and Services Companies, the premier trade body and chamber of commerce of the Tech industry in *India*.
12 KLYNVELD PEAT MARWICK GOERDELER, one of the leading providers of risk, financial services and business advisory, internal audit, and corporate governance in India.

13 A payment option where a customer can make a purchase without having to pay from their own pocket. Generally, customers sign up with a company providing this facility that makes the payment when they make the purchase. However, once the lender pays on the customer's behalf, the customer will have to repay the amount within a stipulated time period.
14 A private company incorporated on August 1, 2019. It is classified as a non-government company. Its authorized share capital is Rs.19,023,800 and its paid-up capital is Rs.15,733,950. It is involved in legal, accounting, book-keeping, and auditing activities; tax consultancy; market research and public opinion polling; business and management consultancy. Directors of Amica Financial Technologies Private Limited are Jitendra Gupta, Vikram Vaidyanathan, and Vishnu Jerome.
15 A tool that provides detailed analysis and reporting of the breakdown of customer's holdings or proposed investments.
16 Artificial intelligence (AI) is the ability of a computer or a robot controlled by a computer to do tasks that are usually done by humans.
17 A whitespace is where the unspoken, unmet needs of customers are discovered in order to spark innovation.
18 Sohini Mitter, 'Fintech Veteran Jitendra Gupta Outlines Jupiter's Vision of Disrupting India's Banking System', July 12, 2021, https://yourstory.com.
19 Praxis Global Alliance is the next-generation management consulting and advisory services firm working with clients across multiple markets and verticals using a practical, grounded, and research-oriented approach.
20 Shishir Mankad, 'Can India's Neobanks Challenge Traditional Lenders and Transform an Archaic Industry?' February 2, 2022, www.thenationalnews.com.
21 A study by NITI Aayog noted, neobanks had much lower cost-to-serve and cost-to-income numbers; per-account operation costs of traditional banks could run up to 10–20 times higher.
22 Sohini Mitter, 'Fintech Veteran Jitendra Gupta Outlines Jupiter's Vision of Disrupting India's Banking System', July 12, 2021, https://yourstory.com.
23 Sohini Mitter, 'Fintech Veteran Jitendra Gupta Outlines Jupiter's Vision of Disrupting India's Banking System', July 12, 2021, https://yourstory.com.

10

UNIFIED PAYMENTS INTERFACE

Revolutionizing Digital Payments in India

Sanjay Fuloria

Synopsis

The Unified Payments Interface, a mobile app-based service in India, enabled transfer of money and payments from several bank accounts of an individual in a convenient manner. It enabled the government effect direct transfer of funds to beneficiaries of several government schemes in a fast and efficient manner, thus preventing problems of leakage of money. It helped the government move closer towards achieving financial inclusion of all sections of the society, especially small traders and the informal sector as well as people in rural India. The developments in technology, the progress made in providing digital infrastructure in the country as well as the availability of mobile phones across the population helped in the implementation of the payment mechanism. While the volume of transactions multiplied over a period of time, there were several instances of frauds which affected many users. Also, there were issues like the absence of a mature governance model and interoperability criteria.

Introduction

Dilip Asbe (Dilip), the MD and CEO of National Payment Corporation of India (NPCI), was looking with satisfaction the progress the organization had made in creating an ecosystem for digital payments in the country. NPCI was set up as an umbrella organization by the Reserve Bank of India (RBI) and Indian Bank's Association to create a robust payment and settlement infrastructure in the country. Within a short period of the launch of the Unified Payments Interface (UPI), by 2022, it had reached a milestone of 10,000 transactions per second.[1]

UPI had solved the problem of financial inclusion and provided a convenient payment system for the citizens and small traders in the country. Dilip had to now work on strengthening

DOI: 10.4324/9781003261155-17

the governance and preventing the possibility of frauds, so that it can scale further and also expand to international payments.

The Launch

On April 11, 2016, Raghuram Rajan, the then Governor of Reserve Bank of India (RBI),[2] inaugurated the United Payments Interface (UPI), a system that could bring several bank accounts into a single mobile application. From August 25, 2016, several banks in the country put their UPI-enabled applications on the Google Play Store.[3] It was a method of linking multiple bank accounts. This link was made through a mobile application. It combined banking capabilities, fund routing, and merchant payments into a single package. This app could also be used to send money from one person to another, from one bank account to another, seamlessly. Individuals and merchants could also make collect requests. This simplified the banking procedure (Figure 10.1) and brought several Indians into the purview of banking.

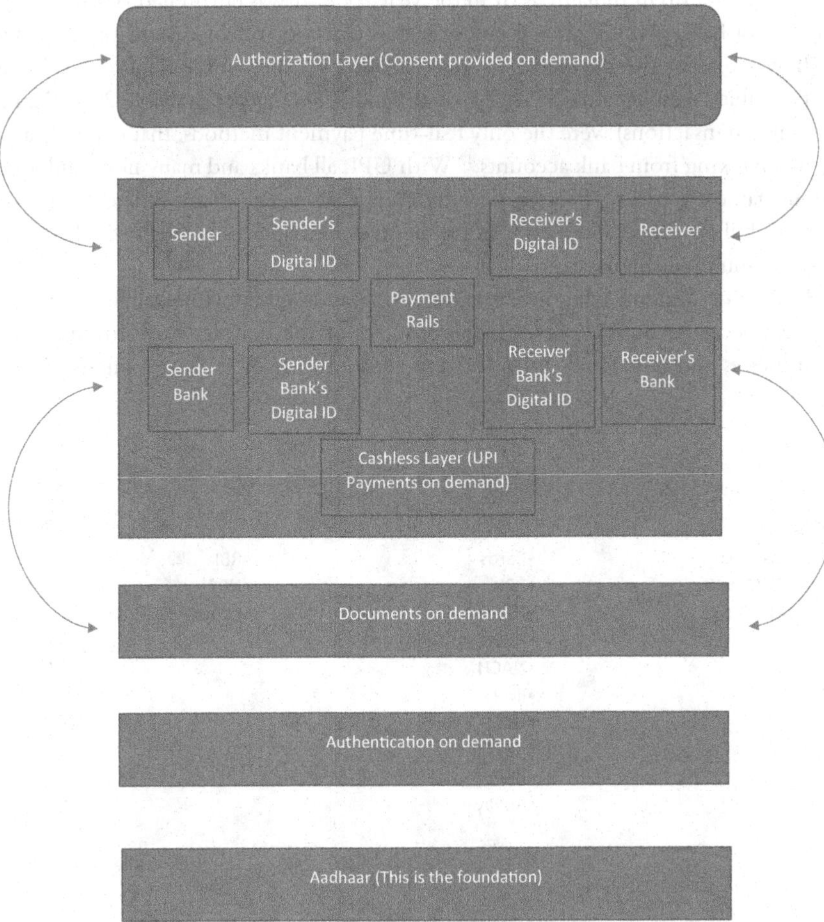

FIGURE 10.1 The UPI process.

Source: Created by the author.

Globally, availability, affordability, and accessibility of digital payment technologies for citizens were considered important. In the year 2011, only 35% of adults in India had a bank account.[4] About 12% adults saved and 8% adults borrowed with a financial institution. These reasons coupled with the anxiety that the private sector may not deliver on this promise forced the government's hand. The Indian Government launched schemes like Pradhan Mantri Jan Dhan Yojna[5] (PMJDY), Atal Pension Yojna[6] (APY), Pradhan Mantri Vaya Vandana Yojana[7] (PMVVY) for the purpose of financial inclusion. RBI helped the financial institutions by creating a network for processing payments.[8] However, as RBI's main role was as a regulator, it subsequently withdrew from this secondary role.

The Reasons for the Launch

SWIFT code[9] was launched in the mid-1970s. This resulted in foreign payment processing, debit, and credit networks replacing intermediaries. Many Indian banks couldn't afford the exorbitant fees charged for payment processing by worldwide intermediaries. A payment corporation was set up in India by RBI in the year 2008. It was christened National Payment Corporation of India (NPCI). It was envisioned as the operator of a multi-payment system. The UPI was one of the payment systems managed by the NPCI (Figure 10.2). Earlier, IMPS[10] (available 24 hours a day, 7 days a week) and RTGS[11] (not available 24 × 7 and only for high-value transactions) were the only real-time payment methods, that could be accessed through net banking from bank accounts.[12] With UPI, all banks and many non-bank financial institutions gained access to peer-to-peer transfers that were instant and round-the-clock. Additionally, bill payments and merchant payments were also possible via a standard platform that supports multiple languages.

The UPI was groundbreaking in several ways: It was designed with mobile in mind, didn't require any special technology, and connected 155 of the country's top institutions. As a result, businesses and individuals in India were allowed to make collect requests. The client

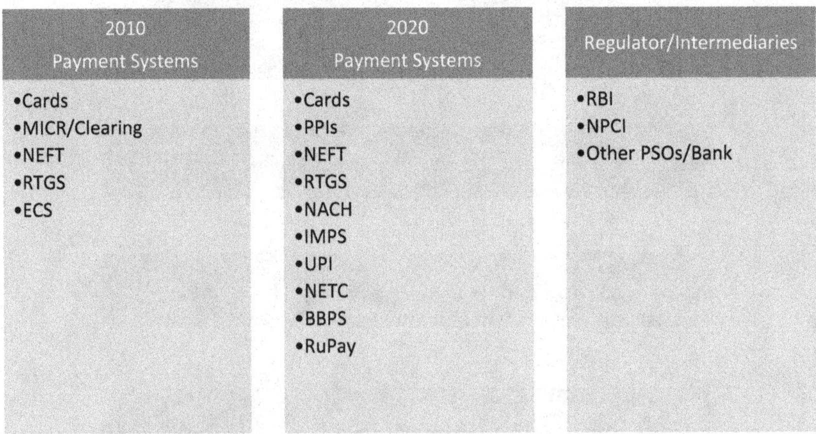

FIGURE 10.2 India's payment systems.[13]

Source: Adapted from 'Journey in the Second Decade of the Millennium,' Payment and Settlement Systems in India, Reserve Bank of India.

who used a tech company's app, namely Google or Amazon, could also communicate with the consumer's bank account. The app was contracted with a bank. The bank, in turn, had a contract with NPCI and was integrated with the UPI switch.

The use of a partially open standard for transactions between these parties aided in the development of trust between UPI and technology companies. There were two standardized improvements over non-availability of open standards and interoperability provided by UPI. These included the need for a standardized interface for entering the Mobile Banking Personal Identification Number (MPIN) and interoperability with the Bharat QR.[14] QR-code format enabled quick and error-free payments at physical places. The MPIN, when combined with a secret code stored on the device, allowed for two-factor authentication without requiring an OTP (One Time Password).

Several app developers had begun to compete on the basis of specialized features. Some platforms, for example, had a 'talk-back' capability to make payments more accessible to people who were visually impaired. It was also accessible to people who couldn't read, and the elderly. Unlike wallets where consumers could store their money inside the app, UPI apps used funds directly from customers' bank accounts. Most UPI apps provided multilingual interfaces similar to BHIMs.[15]

Looking Ahead

While India's approach to solve the problem of financial inclusion via a payments infrastructure was solid in broad strokes, it had a number of major problems, the most important of which was the lack of a mature governance model, interoperability criteria, open standards, and transparent rule-making and enforcement. The payment service provider ecosystem had become less competitive as a result of these challenges. The NPCI's distribution of the BHIM app as a competing mobile app further muddied the waters for local rivals. Following the COVID-19 disruption, a longer-term Mandatory Disclosure Regime (MDR)[16] with proper incentives for all ecosystem actors must be developed.

While it was too early to speculate on the UPI's long-term viability, it was superior to most developed country platforms in terms of access, price, and availability of instant digital payments to hundreds of millions of citizens. The NPCI had established a subsidiary to export the UPI as a technology to other countries as a result of its success. Now, every coin has two sides.

Anything that was successful attracted fraudsters. UPI was no exception. The sheer volume of transactions through UPI was huge. In the month of December 2021, UPI handled transactions worth $111 billion[17] (see Table 10.1). Therefore, it was not surprising that about 80,000 UPI frauds were carried out each month in India, resulting in the voluntary transfer of up to a total of Rs.2 billion by unsuspecting victims. To make matters worse, as the sophistication of these scams increased, there were almost no recourse mechanisms in place. The scamsters used different ways to lure victims. Some instances were 'click to win cashback,' 'call customer care executive from a number listed on the internet to report a problem.'[18] The issue with these frauds was that banks did not recognize these activities as frauds. Payments apps did not have a mandate to report these scams to the NPCI. In most of the cases, the scamsters went scot-free.

UPI was launched by the Government of India with a view to solve the financial inclusion problem. It had served that purpose in conjunction with various other financial inclusion

TABLE 10.1 Volume and Value of Transactions through UPI over the Years

Month	*No. of Banks Live on UPI*	*Volume (in Million)*	*Value (in Rs. Billion)*
December 2021	282	4,566.30	8,268
November 2021	274	4,186.48	7,684
October 2021	261	4,218.65	7,714
September 2021	259	3,654.30	6,543
August 2021	249	3,555.55	6,391
July 2021	235	3,247.82	6,062
June 2021	229	2,807.51	5,474
May 2021	224	2,539.57	4,906
April 2021	220	2,641.06	4,937
March 2021	216	2,731.68	5,049
February 2021	213	2,292.90	4,251
January 2021	207	2302.73	4,312
December 2020	207	2,234.16	4,162
November 2020	200	2,210.23	3,910
October 2020	189	2,071.62	3,861
September 2020	174	1,800.14	3,290
August 2020	168	1618.83	2,983
July 2020	164	1497.36	2,905
June 2020	155	1336.93	2,618
May 2020	155	1,234.50	2,184
April 2020	153	999.57	1,511
March 2020	148	1,246.84	2,065
February 2020	146	1,325.69	2,225
January 2020	144	1305.02	2,162
December 2019	143	1308.4	2,025
November 2019	143	1,218.77	1,892
October 2019	141	1,148.36	1,914
September 2019	141	955.02	1,615
August 2019	141	918.35	1,545
July 2019	143	822.29	1,464
June 2019	142	754.54	1,466
May 2019	143	733.54	1,524
April 2019	144	781.79	1,420
March 2019	142	799.54	1,335
February 2019	139	674.19	1,06,7
January 2019	134	672.75	1,099
December 2018	129	620.17	1,026
November 2018	128	524.94	822
October 2018	128	482.36	750
September 2018	122	405.87	598
August 2018	114	312.02	542
July 2018	114	273.75	518
June 2018	110	246.37	408
May 2018	101	189.48	333
April 2018	97	190.08	270
March 2018	91	178.05	242
February 2018	86	171.4	191
January 2018	71	151.83	156
December 2017	67	145.64	132

Month	*No. of Banks Live on UPI*	*Volume (in Million)*	*Value (in Rs. Billion)*
November 2017	61	105.02	97
October 2017	60	76.96	71
September 2017	57	30.98	53
August 2017	55	16.8	42
July 2017	53	11.63	34
June 2017	52	10.35	31
May 2017	49	9.36	28
April 2017	48	7.2	23
October 2018	128	482.36	750
September 2018	122	405.87	598
August 2018	114	312.02	542
July 2018	114	273.75	518
June 2018	110	246.37	408
May 2018	101	189.48	333
April 2018	97	190.08	270
March 2018	91	178.05	242
February 2018	86	171.4	191
January 2018	71	151.83	156

Source: https://npci.in/what-we-do/upi/product-statistics.

government schemes like Pradhan Mantri Jan Dhan Yojana.[19,20] If UPI can maintain a balance between competitors by having an arm's length regulatory mechanism, it would serve the customers well. There were some negatives attached to the UPI like frauds. Frauds must be stopped. Dilip had to focus on strengthening the governance and preventing the possibility of frauds, so that UPI can scale further and also expand to international payments.

Reflective Questions

1. What do you think is the role played by digital payment systems in our lives?
2. Apart from the convenience that it provides, do you think digital payment systems have increased our propensity to spend?
3. What is your view on the digital payment systems' role in improving financial inclusion in societies?

Suggested Activities

1. Conduct a survey of your friends to assess the impact of digital payment systems in their daily lives and prepare a report.
2. Make an estimate of the amount of cash that you were using for various transactions a few years back and the amount of cash that you use now (because of the use of digital payment systems).

Notes

1 'Internationalization of UPI, Programmable Money, Business Models & New Opportunities with Dilip Asbe, MD & CEO, NPCI', *Prime Venture Partners Podcast*, March 27, 2022, https://primevp.in.

2 Reserve Bank of India is India's Central Bank and a regulatory body for that regulates banking system in the country.
3 'Product Overview', www.npci.org.in/what-we-do/upi/product-overview.
4 Asli Demirgüç-Kunt, Leora Klapper, Dorothe Singer, Saniya Ansar, and Jake Hess, 'The Global Findex Database 2017: Measuring Financial Inclusion and the Fintech Revolution', *World Bank Group*, 2018.
5 Pradhan Mantri Jan Dhan Yojana, a financial inclusion initiative by the Government of India, was launched in 2014. Under this programme, the government aimed to provide banking services to all the households in the country, along with other services like need-based credit, remittances, insurance, and pension.
6 Atal Pension Yojana, is a government-backed pension scheme for people working in the unorganized sector. It was launched in 2015.
7 Pradhan Mantri Vaya Vandana Yojana is an insurance scheme for senior citizens aged 60 years and above.
8 'Unified Payments Will Be as Transformational as Aadhaar', *ET Bureau*, March 23, 2016, https://telecom.economictimes.indiatimes.com/news/unified-payments-interface-will-be-as-transformational-as-aadhaar/51521942.
9 A SWIFT code is a term that defines a universally recognized code used by a financial institution. The code labels a certain financial institution worldwide. It includes from 8 to 11 digits: SWIFT Standards register the code. This code is essentially important if the client wants to transmit funds to another country.
10 Immediate Payment Service is an instant payment inter-bank electronic funds transfer system in India.
11 Real-Time Gross Settlement refers to a funds transfer system that is a process of transferring securities or money between banks on a real-time basis.
12 Sunil Abraham, 'Unified Payment Interface: Towards Greater Cyber Sovereignty', *Observer Research Foundation*, July 13, 2020, www.orfonline.org/research/unified-payment-interface/.
13 ECS: Electronic Clearing Service; PPI: Prepaid Payment Instruments; NACH: National Automated Clearing House; IMPS: Immediate Payment Service; NETC: National Toll Collection Program; BBPS: Bharat Bill Payment System; PSO: Payment System Operator.
14 BharatQR is an integrated payment system in India. It could be used to make Person to Merchant digital payments.
15 BHIM is a mobile payments app based on UPI.
16 Mandatory Disclosure Regime (MDR), EY, www.ey.com/en_uk/tax/mandatory-disclosure-regime.
17 1 US$ = INR74.51 on December 31, 2021.
18 Arundhati Ramanathan, 'The UPI Frauds Undermining India's Payments Fairy Tale', *The Ken*, January 4, 2022, https://the-ken.com/story/the-upi-frauds-undermining-indias-payments-fairytale/?searchTerm=UPI
19 Asli Demirgüç-Kunt, Leora Klapper, Dorothe Singer, Saniya Ansar, and Jake Hess, 'The Global Findex Database 2017: Measuring Financial Inclusion and the Fintech Revolution', *World Bank Group*, 2018
20 International Monetary Fund (IMF), '2019 Article IV Consultation', Country Report No. 19/385, Washington DC, 2019.

PART VII
Sustainability

11

ITC'S E-CHOUPAL 4.0

Harnessing Digital Technologies to Empower Indian Farmers

K.S. Venu Gopal Rao

Synopsis

This case on India-based ITC e-Choupal 4.0 illustrates the manner in which organizations can leverage their learning and experience to build and scale up business models. ITCs e-Choupal model was conceived in the early 2000s as a digital intermediary to empower farmers and create a viable sourcing model for the company as well as enhancing incomes for farmers. The model had matured over the years and contributed to the revenue growth of ITC, one of India's leading diversified conglomerates. This case also describes how ITC moved from the basic sanchalak-driven[1] e-Choupal model to a more inclusive and technology intensive e-Choupal 4.0. The company relied on emerging technologies like artificial intelligence, big data, machine learning, and IoT to create a robust ICT infrastructure that provided Agri-related information and advice in real time to farmers. These interventions were expected to empower farmers by creating better awareness, making agriculture a rewarding profession, bringing them closer to global markets, and ensuring sustainability. Besides, these innovations were also expected to create a larger eco system in the agricultural sector connecting farmers, aggregators, retailers, storage houses, and exporters and importers. ITCs e-Choupal 4.0 could be a game-changer contributing to the Government's plans to double farmer's income by the year 2022. Technological disruptions and digital transformation were expected to change the Agri scenario in the country and empower farmers, and ITC e-Choupal had a major role to play in this transformation.

Introduction

India-based ITC Limited (ITC), a highly diversified Indian conglomerate announced on August 11, 2021, the launch of a mobile based application called MAARS (Metamarket for Advanced Agriculture and Rural Services). This application was part of the larger plan under

DOI: 10.4324/9781003261155-19

the e-Choupal 4.0 initiative[2] that was designed to provide a comprehensive range of personalized services to farmers in the country. Launched after successful pilot testing, the model was designed to share real-time updates on factors that affected farmers directly such as weather and markets, farm diagnostics, monitoring of crops to build weather resilience, agronomic advisory for improving productivity, farm inputs and Agri financial services besides access to local and global output markets.

The scope of e-Choupal 4.0 was holistic and extended beyond farmer benefits. It was also designed to enable plug and play possibilities for new Agri tech companies and put together a range of possibilities that benefited the farmers as well as the companies that joined the ecosystem as collaborators. Company insiders at ITC were confident that this initiative would empower farmers achieve higher productivity and incomes and revolutionize Indian agriculture that trailed its global peers on several performance dimensions.[3] Further, these pioneering initiatives were expected to be the company's contribution to the larger national ambition of doubling farmers income (Dalwai Committee Report 2018).[4]

Indian Agri Sector: Opportunities and Challenges

Agriculture formed the primary source of livelihood for nearly 58% of India's population[5] (IBEF). It contributed to approximately 11%[6] of the global farm output and 20.2% of India's gross domestic product (Ministry of Agriculture).[7] The sector had witnessed sustained growth due to advancements in technology, improvements in seed quality, expansion of irrigation facilities, and ready availability of fertilizers that contributed to improved farmer yields.

According to experts, the sector faced many challenges in all the activities in the value chain from farm to fork. Farmers could not achieve the full potential due to high degree of fragmentation of land holdings according to Ernst & Young report in 2020.[8] Besides, the Agri sector presented a unique paradox. Despite the sector's growth, farmer incomes had not shown marked improvement. They continued to face multiple challenges manifested through stress on limited land availability, depletion of water resources, uncertain climatic conditions, limited awareness of modern farm practices, affordability and usage of advanced Agri tech tools, expensive credit, weak market linkages, and inefficient supply chains as per McKinsey.[9] A report by leading consulting organization Boston Consulting Group (BCG) projected that Indian agriculture needed to catch up with its peers if it had to be competitive and suggested three major areas that had scope for growth, namely farm productivity, farmer profitability, and adoption of new technologies and farming business models.[10]

Experts and consultants however were confident that innovations in Agri technologies, digital transformation investments by many Agri Tech companies as well as the reforms announced from time to time by the Government of India in the last decade could prove to be game-changers and turn around the agricultural sector in India. The resultant outcomes were expected to enhance farmer incomes.[11] For these goals to be achieved, private sector participation in the Agri business sector was necessary.

ITC India Limited

ITC was incorporated in the year 1910 as the Imperial Tobacco Company Limited in Kolkata. The first six decades of the company's existence were devoted to consolidating the cigarettes and tobacco business. The company's name was changed to India Tobacco Company Limited (ITC Limited) in the year 1974.

ITC diversified extensively into many related and unrelated businesses and moved away from its singular dependence on tobacco-based businesses in 2017. The company diversified into FMCG, Hotels, Paperboards, Packaging, Agri Business, and Information Technology. As on March 2021, the company's gross sales value reached Rs.749,790 million, profits were at Rs.130,320 million. It operated with 200 manufacturing units and had 36,500 direct employees (refer to Table 11.1 for operating results of ITC from 2012–2021 and ITC website).[12]

Agri Business Division

The Agri Business Division of ITC was incorporated in the year 1990. During 2021, a significant part of the ITCs revenues (approximately US$1.1 billion) were from the Agri business division. Sanjiv Puri,[13] who took over as Chairman of ITC in May 2018 was convinced that the Agri business division through value-added initiatives had brought stability and margins in a commoditized business of agriculture-based products.[14]

The popular e-Choupal model was an important business line for the Agri business division. ITC Agri was involved in exports of Agri commodities to international markets. Agri products such as soya bean meal, rice, wheat, lentils, marine products, and coffee were exported and earned significant revenues for ITC IBD.[15] The raw material for these had to be procured from the open market. The APMC Act of 1962 mandated companies such as ITC to buy in bulk from government-designated mandis or marketplaces. These marketplaces were controlled by middlemen or agents who held a strong control over the operations at the mandis. The farm to processor route was simple. Farmers had to visit the nearby government-designated mandis with their produce. Usually these were at a considerable distance from their farms.[16] Farmers would then await auctions of the produce to sell their produce at the auction price. Their individual lots were too small to engage in any bargaining with the middlemen and since distances were involved, it was expensive to take the produce back home. Also farmers found it very expensive to ship their produce directly to processors as these were at even longer distances compared to the mandis. Because it was an expensive proposition to ship their small quantities to the processor, farmers found it convenient to complete their transaction at the mandis. The middlemen then aggregated the produce and shipped it to the processors. Companies such as ITC had to procure their requirements from the middlemen. The movement of goods from the farmer to their processors often resulted in long delays, higher procurement costs, and lower realization for farmers. Operating in this highly asymmetric environment resulted in the middlemen profiting at the expense of poor farmers. They would rarely bother about international prices or the quality differences and continued their cycle of exploitation. Since there was no other alternative for farmers or processors, the system continued for a long time. ITC lost its competitiveness in global markets due to the inefficiencies that were beyond its control.

The e-Choupal model was conceived in this backdrop. The company had to make its way through complex regulatory and government machinery to convince the authorities the need for a mechanism to reduce these asymmetries while keeping the spirit of the APMC in place (benefitting farmers). They created a direct channel between the farmer and the processing units to reduce wasteful disintermediation.[17] The farmers could directly deal with the Sanchalak[18] and obtain the rate that prevailed on the day that he wished to sell. The farmer would then go to the ITC hub and get paid instantly. ITC saved on transportation costs (20% less as

TABLE 11.1 Stand-alone Operating Results of ITC Limited for Years 2011–2021

Year Ended 31st March	*FY 2012*	*FY 2013*	*FY 2014*	*FY 2015*	*FY 2016*	*FY 2017*	*FY 2018*	*FY 2019*	*FY 2020*	*FY 2021*
Gross sales value (net of rebates and discounts)	393,530	477,550	538,890	577,990	601,960	641,740	670,820	753,090	760,970	749,790
Gross revenue from sale of products and services	348,720	418,100	467,130	499,650	515,820	550,020	439,570	452,210	463,240	481,510
Total income	360,460	430,440	481,760	519,320	537,140	574,340	464,600	482,690	498,210	517,760
Profit after tax	61,620	74,180	87,850	96,080	93,280	102,010	112,230	124,640	151,360	130,320

All figures in rupees in million.
Source: Company website.

compared to pre-Choupal days), while the farmer saved nearly 50% in transaction costs (refer to Figures 11.1 and 11.2).

e-Choupal 4.0

ITC took advantage of the learning experience of over two decades to scale up the e-Choupal model. The upgraded version was aptly called e-Choupal 4.0. According to the company, this initiative was expected to be a big game-changer. In extending the e-Choupal model and combining it with the disruptive and integrative force of technology, ITC claimed the early mover advantage. It had better infrastructure in place to stage different phases of launch and implement as it moved from the original e-Choupal model to model 4.0 (refer to Table 11.2 for the evolution of the e-Choupal model).

Agriculture all over the world was getting digitally transformed. In fact, a McKinsey report of 2020[19] stated that agriculture would benefit from the combined impact of artificial intelligence, big data, analytics, and sensors that would integrate with other technologies and contribute to increased yields, help conserve precious water resources, and create sustainable agricultural practices across crop cultivation in the entire country. The report projected that the Agri industry in India would add US$500 billion[20] to India's GDP by the year 2030. This contribution would be a 7–9% increase from the levels of farm outputs that were recorded in the year 2020 and help ease a lot of economic pressure piled up on the farmers.

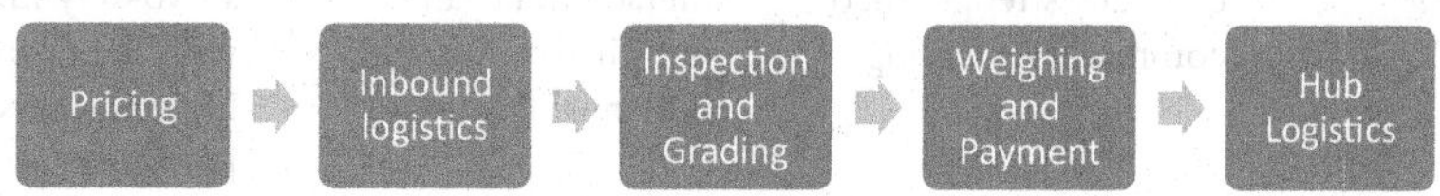

FIGURE 11.1 e-Choupal supply chain (mandi operation process).

Source: World Resources Institute – What Works – ITCs e-Choupal and Profitable Rural Transformation, Michigan Business School, August 2003.

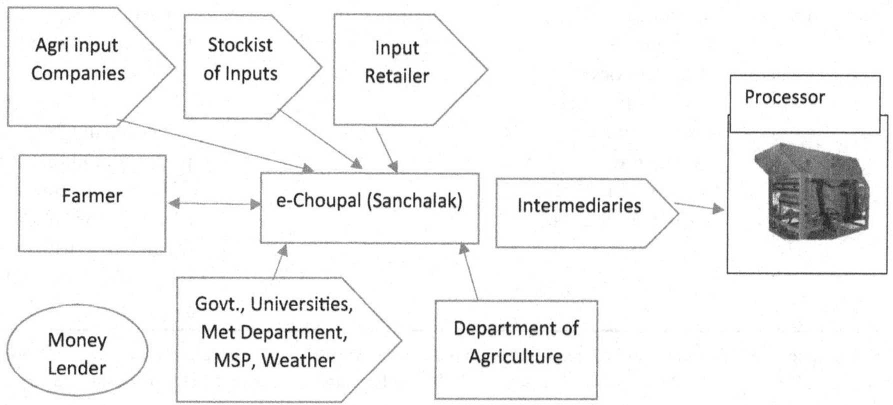

FIGURE 11.2 e-Choupal business model.

Source: B. Bowonder, Vinay Gupta and Amit Singh, 'Developing a Rural Market e-hub – The case study of e-Choupal experience of ITC.'

TABLE 11.2 The Journey of e-Choupal over the Years

Version/Label	*Objectives*	*Benefit to farmers*	*Benefit to ITC*
1.0 Start	To empower small farmers by aggregating them as one large cooperative group of sellers (of produce) and as buyers (of farm inputs)	Farmers could bargain and choose when and what to sell	ITC benefited by direct access to its inputs for its Agri business; it could offer its network to other companies in the value chain
2.0 The Scale Up	To reach 40,000 villages and 4 million farmers. Network offered wider range of services – shared information on weather, price, farming methods, soil testing, cattle care, water harvesting	Greater access to markets, specialized scientific knowledge dissemination leading to superior farm output. Farmers could sell crops to ITCs centres	ITC benefited from greater inclusion and access to farmers on a larger scale. ITC had a channel that began with agriculture but extended into consumer goods and services.
3.0 The Deepening	To add two new anchor businesses – rural jobs and employability and personalized Agri services. Over time the company strengthened commodity sourcing	Farmers had better interaction through Choupal sagars, haats, and through mobile phones. Two way interaction began with the company by individual farmers	ITC could access data from multiple touch points and began using analytics for better prediction. There was a two-way interaction with the farmers. New partners could join the ecosystem. The company laid the foundation for forging a strong relationship with the farmers
4.0 Digital Transformation	To use emerging technologies such as artificial intelligence, machine learning, data analytics, drones, and cutting-edge interventions. The initiative was expected to cover 4 million farmers in ten states	Farmers were provided with customized, contextualized information and services	ITC could leverage from solution integration. It need not rely on the Sanchalaks and Samyojaks.[35] Low-cost last mile reach to the company. New partners could join the ecosystem benefiting ITC earn revenues for network usage by collaborators and partners

Source: Compiled by the author with inputs from www.businesstoday.in/magazine/case-study/story/e-Choupal-version-30-244593-2009-10-23 What works case study – World Resources Institute, Michigan Business School.

S. Siva Kumar (Siva Kumar),[21] head of ITC Agri Business division, described the e-Choupal 4.0 initiative as a platform that would be 'more collaborative and integrated than ever before in leveraging new digital technologies.'[22] He was confident that with e-Choupal 4.0, scaling up to reach a larger farmer base across the country would not be a major challenge. The company could easily add more villages and farmers to the wide network as the need for physical kiosks would wane. He further added that with the projected growth of e-Choupal 4.0, the benefits could reach 10 million farmers by the year 2030. With the government of India pushing for Agri reforms, rapid progress in technological innovations, and the boost for demand-driven agriculture, his targets were well within the projected reach.[23]

Many experts concurred that e-Choupal 4.0 would deliver a gamut of services to the farmers leveraging the power of technology. Unlike the initial version which was primarily aimed at reducing transaction costs and information asymmetry, the latest version would cover many more services. In the words of Siva Kumar, it will assume the role of an 'aggregator of agricultural services' and offer a bouquet of farm-focused services such as crop management, farm mechanization, healthcare, banking, and insurance. In other words, it is a comprehensive platform that offer farm sector–based services.[24] Prototype testing of this model was organized in the states of Maharashtra, Madhya Pradesh, Andhra Pradesh, Karnataka, and Bihar. The e-Choupal 4.0 had a bigger agenda of empowering farmers. Siva Kumar was confident about agriculture's transformative role. He argued that agriculture provided livelihood to 50% of the country's workforce and more opportunities needed to be created to ensure that the next generation of educated Indian farmers would be attracted to sustainable farming activities (refer to Figure 11.3 for e-Choupal 4.0 illustrative model). He suggested that the best way to achieve these goals was to create an ecosystem for agricultural services startups. The emerging model would help provide jobs to the rural youth in agriculture-related services.[25]

Experts agreed that doubling farmer incomes would become the primary driver for motivating next-generation farmers to be educated on the benefits of sustainable farming and the importance of staying connected with their lands. To achieve these goals, the focus had to shift to farmer empowerment. Greater incomes would help reduce income inequalities and create the desired confidence to face economic uncertainties.[26] Siva Kumar was confident that the e-Choupal 4.0 model was a win-win for the company as well as for the farmer. The company benefited from cost reduction of about 10%, while farmer incomes went up between 10% and 25% depending upon region and crop.[27]

Further, Siva Kumar shared the general consensus that the private sector had a pivotal role to play in this transformative effort of linking technology with agriculture. He believed that private sector had to actively engage and supplement government efforts to provide a modern platform for sustainable agricultural services and promote consumption in a shared economy.[28]

Future Challenges

The agriculture sector in India continued to present challenges to policymakers, private sector, government, scientific community, farmers, and related stakeholders.

According to Ashok Dalwai,[29] India succeeded in improving farm yields at the peak of the Green Revolution in the early 1960s.[30] The time had come for this sector to move to the Income Revolution. This required significant improvements in farm productivity and

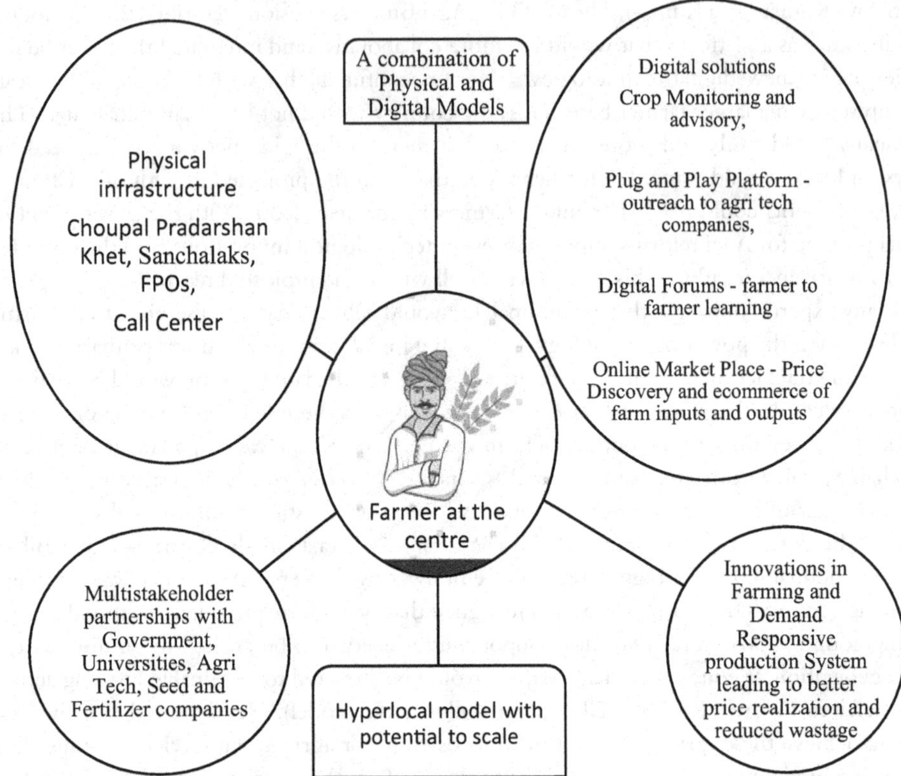

FIGURE 11.3 ITC's e-Choupal 4.0 illustrative model.

Source: Compiled from secondary sources.

reduced costs of production. Disparities in income continued as small farmers continued to be marginalized while affluent farmers with larger landholdings benefited. On an average, the small farmer earned a meagre Rs.6,426 (US$85.41) per month during July 2012 to June 2013 and had to incur expenditure of Rs.6226 (US$82.75) according to Dalwai. There was no possibility for any residual or savings that could be reinvested in this backdrop as the meagre incomes barely helped farmers subsist.[31]

Another significant challenge that the sector faced was in marketing the produce. The APMCs (Agricultural Produce Marketing Committees) that were established in the 1960s had not served their intended purpose and turned into local monopolies exploiting the small and marginal farmers who had to depend on the middlemen at the APMCs. Lack of transparency in pricing led to poorer bargain for the farmers who eventually ended up in the spiral of debts.[32]

The Road Ahead

Infusion of technology in the Agri sector had demonstrated positive returns in India and across the world. Agri industry pioneers in India such as ITC had demonstrated their prowess with business model innovations like e-Choupal 4.0 that led to enhanced productivity in several pilot studies. The system that was managed all these days by manpower had to shift to ICT[33] where technologies such as Geotagging, Geoimagery, drones, and big data would augment the capabilities of existing technology infrastructure. Many companies were investing in this sector attracted by the assurance of returns on their investments.

Farmers needed better information and their mindsets had to change from production orientation to market orientation. This shift was now possible due to digital innovations in agriculture and access to affordable connectivity through mobile phones and other devices.

In the long run, farmer empowerment was expected to hold the key to agricultural sustainability. The e-Choupal model over the years, including the e-Choupal 4.0, demonstrated that large private sector enterprises could combine their social missions with beneficial commercial outcomes. Physical distances, discrimination, and restrictive legislations had kept the small and marginal Indian farmers confined and exposed to the uncertainties for many years. They had virtually no sense of control on their present and future. Experts believed that the e-Choupal model reversed this trend, although the pace of change was gradual. With the e-Choupal 4.0, the diffusion of benefits could be quicker, pervasive, and mutually beneficial for ITC and the farmers. Experts agreed that farmers would be empowered when they had the freedom to control their own destinies and influence the decisions that affected their lives. These changes were also expected to translate into a series of experiences where farmers could learn to see a closer correspondence between their goals and a sense of how to achieve them.[34] ITC Agri seemed to emerge as the most significant beneficiary from these changes. Creating the mobile application (MAARS) was the beginning point in ITCs attempt to scale up connectivity and present a host of services to farmers under e-Choupal 4.0. How should they spread the awareness about the potential advantages? Could the existing Sanchalaks (lead villagers) augment this requirement? If not, what available alternatives could be explored?

Reflective Questions

1. What is the role of Government and private sector in leveraging the extensive capabilities of digital transformation in the agricultural sector in India? How can collaborators such as Universities, Independent R&D organizations, and Agri Tech companies contribute to the growth and development of the vast ecosystem?
2. Farmer empowerment depends on economic empowerment. Discuss how the e-Choupal 4.0 will help achieve the stated objectives of farmer empowerment in India.

Activity

Work on the following questions in teams of two prior to the actual case discussion and prepare brief reports.

a. Compare and contrast the Agri-based Value Chains in the two most populous countries of the world, namely India and China. What fundamental differences exist in the value chains? Analyse the extent to which technology has disrupted the sector in both the countries.
b. Identify and compare two inclusive Agri business models that you are aware of. What are the similarities and differences?

Notes

1 Sanchalak: the lead villager who is computer literate and trained by ITC to assist farmers. The Sanchalak's house is connected to the Internet.
2 ITC Website – www.itcportal.com/businesses/agri-business/e-choupal.aspx.
3 ITC Website – www.itcportal.com/businesses/agri-business/e-choupal.aspx.
4 The Government of India appointed an eight-member inter-ministerial committee in April 2016 to prepare a blueprint for doubling farmer incomes by 2022. The company was headed by Ashok Dalwai, Additional Secretary Department of Agriculture, Cooperation and Farmers' Welfare. The final report was submitted to the Government of India on September 17, 2018.
5 www.ibef.org/industry/agriculture-india.aspx (accessed November 20, 2021), IBEF – India Brand Equity Foundation.
6 www.mckinsey.com/industries/agriculture/our-insights/how-digital-innovation-is-transforming-agriculture-lessons-from-india.
7 Press Information Bureau, 'Ministry of Agriculture and Farmer's Welfare', August 3, 2021, www.pib.gov.in/PressReleasePage.aspx?PRID=1741942.
8 AgriTech – Towards Transforming Indian Agriculture, Ernst &Young India Report, 2020.
9 BCG report – Harvesting Golden Opportunities in Indian Agriculture: From Food Security to Farmer's Income Security by 2025.
10 Shaping India's Future Together, https://media-publications.bcg.com/bcg-shaping-indias-future-together.pdf.
11 AgriTech – Towards Transforming Indian Agriculture, Ernst & Young India Report 2020.
12 www.itcportal.com/about-itc/index.aspx.
13 Sanjiv Puri, Managing Director, ITC since May 2018.
14 How ITC is churning value from its highly commoditized Agri business division, Business Today.in, November 13, 2021.
15 ITC IBD: The International Business Division of ITC.
16 APMC Act of 1962 – required companies such as ITC to buy from government-designated mandis (marketplace) only.
17 Ali Farhoomand, *ITC e-Choupal: Corporate Social Responsibility in Rural India: Asia Case Research Center.* The University of Hong Kong, Hong Kong, 2008.
18 Sanchalak: the lead villager who is computer literate and trained by ITC to assist farmers. The Sanchalak's house is connected to the internet.
19 Agriculture's Connected Future: How Technology Can Yield Growth, McKinsey Report, October 2020.
20 One US$ = Rs.75.24 (as on December 6, 2021).
21 S Siva Kumar, Head of IT and Agri Businesses at ITC.
22 ITC sees e-Choupal 4.0 deliver early gains; focus shifts to expanding geographical footprint, Business Today.in, www.businesstoday.in/latest/corporate/story/itc-sees-e-choupal-40-deliver-early-gains-focus-shifts-to-expanding-geographical-footprint-239860–2019–11–25.
23 'After Helping ITC Cut Costs, Now e-Choupal Model Set for an Upgrade', *Business Standard,* June 22, 2020.
24 https://krishijagran.com/news/e-choupal-40-by-mid-2019-a-mobile-version-to-multiply-farmers-income/.
25 'ITC Turns Aggregator with e-Choupal 4.0 to Boost Farm Income', *Business Standard,* June 2017.
26 'Empowering Farmers Is Important', *Economic Times*, August 2019, https://economictimes.indiatimes.com/news/economy/agriculture/view-empowering-farmers-is-important/articleshow/70599800.cms.
27 'Farmers Have Earned Up to 50% More via e-Choupal', *Business Standard,* October 2020.
28 'After Helping ITC Cut Costs, Now e-Choupal Model Set for an Upgrade', *Business Standard,* June 22, 2020.
29 Ashok Dalwai was the CEO, National Rainfed Area Authority, Ministry of Agriculture, Government of India and Chairman of the Committee appointed by the Government of India to submit a report on Doubling Farmer Incomes by 2022.
30 The Green Revolution in India was the pioneering work of agriculture scientists and farmers that began in the early 1950s and extended up to 1985–1986. Dramatic improvements in yields were achieved in the agricultural sector.

31 TimetoExploreTech,Outlook,2017,www.outlookindia.com/newsscroll/time-to-explore-tech-policy-shift-of-green-revolution-to-new/985564.

32 How Digital Innovation Is Transforming Agriculture: Lessons from India. McKinsey Report, 2019.

33 ICT – Internet and Communication Technologies.

34 Marc A Zimmerman, 'Psychological Empowerment: Issues and Illustrations', *American Journal of Community Psychology, 23*(5) (1995).

35 *Sanchalaks*: the person in whose home the personal computer was installed. Farmers would access the information on prices and commodities from the Sanchalaks. *Samyojaks* were the commission agents who earned income from ITC by providing logistical services in the absence of formal infrastructure in remote areas.

Additional References and Supplemental Readings

'Annual Report of the Department of Agriculture, Cooperation and Farmer's Welfare, 2020–21', https://agricoop.nic.in/sites/default/files/Web%20copy%20of%20AR%20%28Eng%29.pdf.

'Decoding Agriculture in India and the Covid-19 Crisis, Grant Thornton – FICCI Report', June 2020, https://ficci.in/spdocument/23267/FICCI-GT-Report-on-Agriculture.pdf.

'From Agriculture to AgTech', An Industry Transformed – Monitor Deloitte Research, 2016.

'Market Provisioning of Technology Enabled Agriculture Services in India, World Bank Group, South Asia Agriculture and Rural Growth Discussion Note Series', March 2020, https://openknowledge.worldbank.org/handle/10986/34714.

Narayanamoorthy, A., 'Farm Income in India: Myths and Realities', *Indian Journal of Agricultural Economics, 72*(1) (2017), 49–75.

Saiz-Rubio, V., & Rovira-Mas, F., 'From Smart Farming towards Agriculture 5.0: A Review on Crop Data Management', *Agronomy, 10* (2017).

Shilomboleni, H., Pelletier, B., & Gebru, B., 'ICT4Scale in Smallholder Agriculture: Contributions and Challenges – Research Report', *16* (2020), 47–65.

'Transforming Agriculture through Digital Technologies, Deloitte Report', January 2020, https://www2.deloitte.com/gr/en/pages/consumer-business/articles/transforming-agriculture-through-digital-technologies.html.

PART VIII

Inclusive Businesses

12

UNILEVER PAKISTAN

Creating a Gender-balanced Business

Rupali Chaudhuri

> *The business case for gender equality and diversity has long been accepted as an integral part of organizations across the world. In Pakistan, we too are defining the organizational road map that will empower women to become the flag-bearers of economic success.*
>
> –*Shazia Syed, Chairperson & CEO, Unilever Pakistan*[1]

Synopsis

This case highlights Unilever Pakistan's practice of creating a gender-balanced business. The results from the Global Gender Gap Report 2021 ranked Pakistan 153rd out of the 156 countries. Even in such a scenario, there were some companies like Unilever, which strived for gender balance in their business. This case focuses on the policies, practices at Unilever Pakistan, aimed at helping women employees. In line with Unilever's long held slogan, 'Feel good, look good and get more out of life,' all team members played a pivotal role in shaping the workforce at Unilever. The case describes how developing a gender-balanced business is important, how it translates into improved operational results and discusses the challenges in creating and sustaining a gender-balanced organization.

Introduction

The Global Gender Gap Index, a framework used extensively by the World Economic Forum to ascertain the gender-based disparities across the globe, tracks disparities on four key areas: economic participation and opportunity; educational attainment; health and survival; and political empowerment. The Global Gender Gap Report 2021 ranked Pakistan 153rd out of the 156 countries[2] (see Table 12.1). Only Iraq, Yemen, and Afghanistan fared worse. However, there was improvement noted with more women taking on professional and technical roles – 25.3% up from 23.4% in the previous edition of the Global Gender Gap

DOI: 10.4324/9781003261155-21

TABLE 12.1 Ranking of Countries: Global Gender Gap Report

South Asia			
Country	*Rank*		*Score*
	Regional	*Global*	
Bangladesh	1	65	0.719
Nepal	2	106	0.683
Sri Lanka	3	116	0.67
Maldives	4	128	0.642
Bhutan	5	130	0.639
India	6	140	0.625
Pakistan	7	153	0.556
Afghanistan	8	156	0.444

Source: https://www3.weforum.org/docs/WEF_GGGR_2021.pdf

Report 2020.[3] While the number of women professionals in Pakistan was low compared to several South Asian countries, there were a few organizations that had fared well in employing women professionals. One such company was the Anglo Dutch FMCG major Unilever Pakistan Limited (Unilever Pakistan). 'The media projects Pakistan as conservative, but there is a large segment of society that is liberal and broad minded,' said Ehsan Malik, former country manager for Unilever Pakistan.[4]

Unilever Pakistan was well known in the Pakistani corporate circle for its commitment for gender diversity. The company's long held slogan, 'Feel good, look good and get more out of life,' encouraged all team members to play a pivotal role in shaping the workforce at Unilever. The company made an effort to recruit women employees and retain them in order to unlock their hidden potential. Unilever was able to differentiate itself from their peers by their employee-centric HR practices. These practices made the organization the number 1 employer of choice.[5] Over the years, the organization created a culture of high empowerment, high engagement that resulted in a satisfied workforce. The organization looked for opportunities where it would invest in its employees. It had become a model on gender balance in spite of the bad press due to the ranking in the World Economic Forum.

Background Note

Analysts pointed out from the Global Gender Gap Report 2021 that Pakistan's gender gap widened by 0.7 percentage points to 55.6%. The Report further placed the country at 152 in economic participation and opportunity; 144 in educational attainment; 153 in heath and survival; and 98 in political empowerment. The report commented that fewer women participate in the total labour force (22.6%) and even a very few were in the managerial position (4.9%). This indicated that there were large income disparities between men and women. The report further stated that the income of a Pakistani woman was 16.3% of a man's.[6]

Unilever Pakistan Limited, a fast-moving consumer goods (FMCG) company based in Karachi,[7] Pakistan was formerly known as Lever Brothers Pakistan Limited. This company at Pakistan was a subsidiary of Conopco Inc. USA,[8] whereas its ultimate parent company was Unilever N.V. Netherlands. As of 2021, the Unilever Pakistan had its manufacturing facilities

TABLE 12.2 Financial Revenue

	Half Year Ended, June 30, 2020 *	*Half Year Ended June 30, 2019**	*Increase %*
Net sales	7,670,039	6,535,224	17.4%
Profit before taxation	1,908,833	1,382,159	38.1%
Profit after taxation	1,726,317	953,134	81.1%
Earnings per share	271	150	81.1%

* Expressed in Thousands.
Currency: Pakistani rupee.
Source: https://assets.unilever.com/files/92ui5egz/production/31275868c8647a9fe4d273b2d29bf9796246b37d.pdf/condensed-interim-financial-statements-for-the-half-year-ended-30-june-2020.pdf

in Lahore and sales offices spread across the country. The company offered a wide range of consumer and commercial food products under the brand names of Rafhan,[9] Knorr,[10] Energile,[11] and Glaxose-D[12] and food solutions. As of June 30, 2020, the sales stood at US$43.648 million[13] and earnings per share increased by 81.1%[14] versus the same period as of June 30, 2019 (refer to Table 12.2).

Practices

In 2010, the parent company Unilever N.V. Netherlands set a target to achieve 50/50 gender balance in their managerial roles across their global business by 2020. Back in 2010, women accounted for 38% of their managerial roles.[15] The leadership team wanted to introduce a number of programmes so that women employees could be better supported in the organization. While the organization's policies were globally aligned, each Unilever company had the flexibility to find the best mix between global and local policies. Unilever understood the importance of catering to the local Pakistani society's cultural and social beliefs and practices.

Companies usually tailored each policy according to the local culture, specific business needs, and business environment. In 2017, Unilever Pakistan reaffirmed its commitment towards gender diversity by signing onto the women's empowerment principles with support from the UN Women (United Nations Entity for Gender Equality and the Empowerment of Women). These principles were a set of guidelines that helped organizations across the globe in promoting gender equality in the workplace, marketplace, and community.

Unilever reported on March 3, 2020, that women occupied nearly 50% of management positions globally. Women made up 50% of its finance managers, 47% of its operations and technology managers. Its supply chain managers comprised 40% women.[16] CEO Alan Jope mentioned, 'Diversity & Inclusion is one of the three things that we want Unilever to be famous for,' and further added that 'This means making sure our business is fair, attracting and retaining the very best talent and helping them unlock their full potential.'[17]

One of the ways Unilever Pakistan achieved its gender balancing targets was by recruiting female engineers in their remote factories. The company provided security-guard staffed housing for these female engineers, thereby reassuring their families about their safety.

Unilever Pakistan realized early on how important the facilities were to help employees bring out their best productivity. In view of this, the organization set up day care facilities in their office buildings for young parents, especially women employees in 2004.[18] The facilities were run by professionals with vast experience in running child care facilities. These facilities helped working mothers focus on their work and careers.

In order to provide financial support for female candidates who aspired a career in management, Unilever Pakistan started a scholarship in partnership with the Lahore University of Management Sciences. This scholarship was open to women belonging to underprivileged background whose family earnings were less than Pakistani rupee 25,000 a month.[19]

Unilever Pakistan had been offering flexi-working hours since 2009. Under this system, employees were given an option to select one of three timeslots for their work to be done with the consent from their line managers.[20]

Shattering the Gender Stereotype

Unilever Pakistan worked to create awareness on prejudiced stereotyping, while working closely with the UN Women. This partnership aimed at eliminating archaic portrayal of women and men in the workplace, especially in advertisements.[21] In 2018, the company celebrated International Women's Day by urging employees to challenge the unfair portrayal of the social norms of men and women in the workplace. One such employee was Faizah Khan (Faizah). She was hired in 2017 as the first female area sales manager in Pakistan in a male-dominated workforce and customers. Unilever Pakistan encouraged more women coming into the field sales area by providing them with an improved washroom facility, day care for children, and female-friendly distribution centres. Due to these facilities Faizah, a young mother was able to meet the challenges of family commitments and work responsibilities head on. She believed in being true to herself and doing her job diligently. This helped her to gain respect and trust from the male peers. She said:

> This has been enlightening for both male and female colleagues. They can see a work – life balance is attainable and nothing can stop a woman working in sales. My gender does not stop me doing my job well, and it's great to see lot of my work colleagues and retailers recognising that women have enough potential to handle a field job in parallel with managing their family lives.[22]

Guddi Baaji

In sync with Unilever's global strategy to move into the beauty business, one of the business strategies that Unilever Pakistan famously adopted was the Guddi Baaji[23] programme. In Pakistan, two-thirds of the population lived in rural areas where people were conservative and women did not interact with men. Women were reluctant to shop for beauty products in shops manned by men. In order to make the women aware of the different beauty products and ease the process of buying those products, Unilever hired 2,000 women from rural and low-income areas and trained them in basic beauty skills (how to blow dry hair, apply bridal make up) for three months.[24] These women later established salons at their home towns where different rural women would visit them for beauty treatments and also to buy products. This was one of the ways in which Unilever Pakistan had reached out to the rural population.

In 2019, the company partnered with JazzCash[25] and trained more than 8,000 women as entrepreneurs, focusing on how to run profitable businesses.[26] The aim of this partnership was to increase the value for their products and drive financial inclusion for the lower income women in Pakistan. As Shazia Syed (Shazia) added:

> The 'Guddi Baaji' initiative empowers rural women by enhancing livelihoods and increasing influence within their communities. We are breaking gender stereotypes and creating role models. I am confident that our partnership with Jazz will increase opportunities for women in rural Pakistan through the power of mobile.[27]

An internal survey conducted by Unilever Pakistan reported that over 40% of Guddi Baajis had smartphones and they used these with proficiency. They were able to place orders and make payment online. This helped these women achieve financial empowerment and independence.

Corporate Board and Management Councils

Industry experts believed that participation of women in corporate boards had a positive impact on a company's profits and could also broaden the market presence. At Unilever Pakistan, Shazia was appointed as Chairman and CEO in November 2015.[28] She was the only female member on the board (in office from November 2015 to February 2020). She was responsible for spearheading the growth in Pakistan in all the Unilever's categories. A critical milestone for Shazia had been the successful completion of the US$120 million project to expand manufacturing capacity.[29] She had been a strong advocate for gender diversity in the workforce and played a key role in launching the first women empowerment awards in 2018.[30] In February 2020, the board appointed Asima Haq (Asima) as part of the local management council. Asima was the Director, Beauty and Personal Care. In the same month, the company announced change in their senior leadership and appointed Amir Paracha (Amir) as Chairman and CEO, while Shazia was appointed as the Executive Vice President for Unilever's global tea business, based in the Netherlands. Amir was a veteran at Unilever and had been pivotal in reshaping sales and marketing across North Africa and Middle East business. As a vice president for customer development, Amir had been instrumental in leading the digital transformation agenda at Unilever. He championed many projects, including inclusion and well-being in Unilever.

Looking Ahead

Two events during 2020 and beyond created uncertainties for organizations in Pakistan.

The COVID-19 outbreak led to unprecedented disruption worldwide, Unilever Pakistan was no exception. The company needed to understand the behavioural changes of consumers and at the same time ensure safety of their employees. The company employed nearly 21,000 people across Pakistan.[31] They had seven factories and around 8,000 salesmen who worked alongside their 400 distributors. These salesmen would meet different retailers in person and book orders. Due to the movement restrictions and while maintaining social distancing, many salesmen were not able to receive orders and get them fulfilled through the distributors. In order to combat challenges due to COVID-19, Amir and the leadership team prioritized safety. They followed the four-tier safety system which included no travel by public transport, temperature checks at the factory, and lunch divided into three shifts to enable social distancing. The company had started the work from home (WFH) for some of their functions. Amir observed and remarked in an interview:

> I did not think I would be running such a huge organisation remotely for the last five weeks. Of course, different people have different experiences and some have found it a bit overwhelming because a lot of the stuff we had previously outsourced, we now have to do ourselves.[32]

The company took a number of stringent measures like reducing the number of operating hours from five to two and providing employees with masks, sanitizers, and gloves in order to reduce the spread.

Apart from this, one of the bigger challenges Pakistan was facing was the economic crisis. The stringent economic conditions laid out by IMF and the conditions imposed by the Saudi government resulted in a weakened Pakistani rupee, rising inflation, and a heavy trade deficit. Due to these economic conditions, the country has been forced to increase taxes. Fuel prices surged and electricity became more expensive. Industry experts opined that this economic crisis would have an adverse impact on the fast-moving consumer goods companies. As raw material costs would increase, higher rate of interest for investments was expected to have a detrimental impact on the margins. Analysts opined that the liquidity crisis in Pakistan would eventually lead to a plunge in the consumer spending as people would down-trade. It remained to be seen how Unilever Pakistan would handle the turbulence and weather the economic storm.

Unilever Pakistan had refined its gender-balanced business model through time. It would be interesting to see if this balance can be maintained in the near future, especially when a company had a varied workforce and future leaders must recognize and encourage cultural differences.

Research scholars opined that an increase in women participation was positively and significantly correlated to firm profitability.[33] Industry experts noted the appointment of women employees at Unilever Pakistan and opined that further analysis was needed to check if this correlation holds true or not and how such a relation can be utilized to bring in more revenues and market share, product portfolio. Will Amir be able to bring more women on the senior leadership roles and thereby increase revenues?

Through the COVID crisis, companies had faced many challenges like lack of authentic information, limited resources, and technology gaps, but one of the bigger challenges would be how businesses will function in the 'next normal.' Industry experts analysed data and commented that many companies were pulling back on diversity initiatives as there were bigger challenges ahead. In light of the uncertainties, Amir had to set his agenda to lead the organization amidst these challenges and also continue on the path of gender balance and diversity. Will Amir and his team thrive in the 'next normal'?

Reflective Questions

1. How would you evaluate Unilever Pakistan's initiatives for building a gender-balanced organization?
2. Why is the issue of gender balance in workforce important for Unilever Pakistan?

3. What are the common challenges faced by Unilever Pakistan and how did the organization overcome these challenges through their practices?
4. What are the challenges faced by the new CEO? What should he do to ensure the continuance of the practices?

Learning Activities

Pick an organization in your country and study the status of gender balance and diversity in this organization. Try to analyse the factors that have contributed to the status.

Notes

1 'Unilever Pakistan and UN Women collaborate for the Economic Empowerment of Women', December 12, 2017, www.asiapacific.unwomen.org.
2 Amin Ahmed, 'Pakistan Loses Two Spots on Global Gender Gap Index, Slides into Ranks of Worst Four Countries', March 31, 2021, www. dawn.com.
3 'Global Gender Gap Report 2021', www. weforum.org.
4 Avivah Wittenberg-Cox, 'Unilever's Pakistan Country Manager on Promoting More Women', January 22, 2013, www.hbr.org.
5 'We Are Unilever', www.unilever.pk/our-company.
6 'Global Gender Gap Report 2021', www.weforum.org.
7 Karachi is a premier industrial and financial centre of Pakistan and is located in the province of Sindh.
8 Conopco Inc. does business as Unilever and provides personal care products like perfumes, soaps, and shampoos.
9 Rafhan is one of the biggest food brands in Pakistan dealing with corn oil, cornflour, custard, ice cream, jelly, and pudding.
10 Knorr is a food brand dealing with Knorr chicken noodles and soup.
11 Energile is a food brand dealing with energy drinks.
12 Glaxose-D is a food brand dealing with non-flavoured energy drink.
13 1 Pakistani rupee is US$0.0057. The sales 7,670 million Pakistan rupee stands at US$43.648 million.
14 'Unilever Pakistan Foods Limited', June 30, 2020, www.assets.unilever.com.
15 'Half of This Company's 14,000 Managers Are Women', March 3, 2020, www.businesstoday.in.
16 Katie Clarey, 'Unilever Announces Gender Parity Among Global Managers', March 10, 2020, www.hrdive.com.
17 'Nine Ways We're Making Unilever a More Gender-Balanced Business', March 9, 2020, www. unilever.pk.
18 'Unilever Sets Up Childcare Centre', February 28, 2004, www.fp.brecorder.com.
19 Palgrave Macmillan Ltd, *The Grants Register 2016: The Complete Guide to Postgraduate Funding Worldwide*. Palgrave Macmillan UK, United Kingdom, 2016a.
20 Mustafa Nemat, 'Unilever Tries Out "Agile Working"', September 6, 2010, www.tribune.com.pk.
21 'Unilever – Jazz Cash Guddi Baji Livelihoods Program', September 9, 2021, www.unilever.pk.
22 "Everyday Actions Our Employees Are Taking to Smash Gender Stereotypes', March 8, 2018, www.unilever.com.
23 Guddi Baaji means in the local Urdu language good sister.
24 Avivah Wittenberg-Cox, 'Unilever's Pakistan Country Manager on Promoting More Women', January 22, 2013, www.hbr.org.
25 JazzCash is a Pakistani mobile financial services provider.
26 'Unilever – Jazz Cash GuddiBaji Livelihoods Program', September 9, 2021, www.unilever.pk.
27 Mehtab Haider, 'Corporate Sector to Empower Women Through "GuddiBaji' Programme"', December 13, 2017, www.thenews.com.pk.
28 'Five Female Pakistani CEOs Breaking Barriers', March 8, 2018, www.geotv.com.
29 'Unilever Pakistan Limited Announces Change in Leadership', January 15, 2020, www.unilever.pk.

30 Anusha Sachwani, 'Unilever Pakistan CEO Shazia Syed Exits, Amir Paracha to Take Over', January 16, 2020, www.brandsynario.com.
31 Mariam Ali Baig, 'Strategising for a Post Covid-19 Portfolio', July 2020, www.aurora.dawn.com.
32 Ibid.
33 Rey Đặng, L'Hocine Houanti, Krishna Reddy, and Michel Simioni, 'Does Board Gender Diversity Influence Firm Profitability? A Control Function Approach', *Economic Modelling, 90* (2020), 168–181, www.sciencedirect.com/science/article/pii/S0264999319306649.

PART IX

Businesses Promoting Gender Equality in Society

13

SHUTTLE

Fearless Drive

S.S.M. Sadrul Huda, Ishtiake Uddin, Afsana Akhtar, and Segufta Dilshad

Synopsis

This case presents the day-to-day struggle women in Bangladesh faced in travelling by public transport and how some companies were trying to fix the problem. The case focuses mainly on an app-based company 'Shuttle' that provided safe transportation facilities for women. With cases of sexual harassment increasing, women in Dhaka city needed to be wary of using public spaces such as roads, sidewalks, and parks. The city was considered 'not women-friendly,' according to Action Aid. About 53% of women in Dhaka city did not favour venturing out of their homes due to the lack of a safe transport system. In this case, three significant issues in the transportation sector from the perspective of a woman are discussed: the state of public transportation for female passengers and the necessary steps that stakeholders such as the government, owners of vehicles, educational institutions, and women themselves should take. The availability of safe transport was critical as the number of working women grew. Women also needed a reliable, easy-to-use, accessible mode of transport to travel regularly for other chores. Finally, routes outside major commuter corridors were unavailable during off-peak hours, when women were more likely to require public transportation to reach their social and economic networks.

In this situation, an app-based ride-sharing company named Shuttle tried to address the problems the women in Dhaka were facing. This organization provided a women-only transportation system in comfortable, air-conditioned vehicles and an expert trip manager to supervise the journey. The organization gave utmost priority to the safety and comfort of the passengers. Most importantly, it saved women from the living nightmare they had to go through in the form of sexual harassment in public transport.

DOI: 10.4324/9781003261155-23

Introduction

Every day, like women worldwide do, women in Dhaka, the capital of Bangladesh in South Asia, had to report to work on time. However, the city's women faced different challenges that their global counterparts did not. Many women reported that travelling by public transportation was nothing less than a nightmare and was akin to a minor battle.

While boarding public transport (i.e. bus/train) was a challenge due to the massive crowds, women who finally managed to board the bus/train faced harassment from men, who abused them verbally and pushed them.

According to Ministry of Public Administration data, as of 2021, women accounted for 27% of all government employees, up from 21% in 2014. The country's overall workforce was approximately 69 million.[1] According to the data, women made up 30.4% of the workforce in 2021.

Public Transport and Women in Bangladesh

In Bangladesh, many female passengers reported being physically or mentally assaulted by drivers or male passengers when riding at night. Over the years, torture and harassment had escalated due to a lack of faith in law enforcement and social ignorance. According to an Action Aid[2] report, many female passengers in Bangladesh's major cities faced various types of harassment, including sexual harassment. In their study, 42% of female bus riders reported sexual harassment by male co-passengers. Women reported being sexually harassed by transport officials in 53% of cases. According to a BRAC[3] poll, 94% of women in the country faced violence on public transport. Incidents that attracted attention included one on February 13, 2014, when a little girl was raped on a bus in Manikganj.[4] On May 12, 2015, a textile worker was raped on a moving bus in Sonargaon,[5] Narayanganj, and subsequently died after she was pushed out of the moving vehicle. On January 23, 2018, five bus drivers raped two sisters in Barisal.[6] On August 25, 2018, a marketing assistant in Mymensingh[7] was raped inside a bus. Her body was later found in the Madhupur forest. On January 6, 2016, three bus workers raped a teenager in Nandail, Mymensingh.[8] According to the Passenger Welfare Association, 59 women were raped or sexually assaulted while using public transport in 2019. Sadly, these were only the reported figures. Every day, hundreds of unreported incidents took place.

Overall, such incidents created a sense of fear among women about taking public transport for their daily commute. In Bangladesh, where equal rights and participation of men and women were stressed, women's safety in public transit became a huge concern. Public transit in Bangladesh was not considered 'mobility just'[9] because one gender suffered more than the other. Dhaka, the capital, was one of South Asia's least motorized cities, with 30 motorized vehicles per 1,000 people as of 2005. As a result, daily bus travel was characterized by congestion, delays, and poor traffic management.

Existing Transportation Options for Women

A study by BRAC titled 'Sexual Harassment of Women and Accident-Free Roads' found that 94% of women in the country were subjected to verbal, physical, or other forms of sexual harassment while travelling on public transport.[10]

Separate public transport for women passengers was introduced in Dhaka in 2010. Bangladesh Road Transport Corporation (BRTC) launched 22 buses exclusively for women. However, due to the COVID-19 pandemic, the operation of those buses was stopped. Even after the pandemic-related restrictions were lifted, the buses did not return to the roads. As of 2021, only four buses meant exclusively for women were plying. In this situation, women continued to travel like they had been doing all the while facing the same problems they always had.

Dolonchapa

Along with BRTC, in 2016, transport company Dolonchapa launched the first private bus service for women from Mirpur-12 to Motijheel. Road Transport and Bridges Minister Obaidul Quader inaugurated the 'Dolonchapa' AC bus service.

The Dolonchapa women-only bus service was launched in June 2020 by Rangs Group and Volvo Eicher Commercial Vehicles. The Rangs Group of Companies (RGC) was widely recognized as one of Bangladesh's most successful businesses. The company was an early innovator in the country's electronics and electrical goods market. The service proved to be a boon to women travelling on two routes – from ECB Chattar to Azimpur and Mirpur 12 to Motijheel.

The Dolonchapa bus service was extended to Dhaka, bringing some relief to women who used public transport in the capital city. Each Dolonchapa bus had 36 seats, with nine reserved for physically challenged and pregnant women. It was also equipped with four CCTV cameras, a fire extinguisher, and a first-aid box.

In 2019, the number of Dolonchapa buses stood at four. Authorities then said the number of buses would gradually be increased. However, in reality, the opposite happened. The 'Dolanchampa' bus was rarely seen in the capital as of 2021.

ZoBike

ZoBike was an app-based bicycle rental service for both men and women. It also served the purpose of providing secure, harassment-free transportation. After all, if a woman could ride a bicycle, she did not need to use any other public transport. Women could log in to the app and see if any bikes were available in their area. Once they found a cycle, they had to book it and get it at the appointed time. They had to return the cycle once they had finished their transportation-related activities for the day. The problem with this app was that it was limited to serving only women who could ride bicycles, which most women could not do.

Finding a Solution

Every problem creates market demand, and when there is a demand, marketers find an opportunity to fulfil that demand through their value propositions. Just after graduation, the founders of Shuttle – Jawad Jahangir, Riasat Chowdhury, and Shah Sufian Mahmud Chowdhury – saw that women were facing problems while travelling by public transport. They realized it was high time someone did something to help women travel without any trouble.

So, not only to fulfil a rising demand and enhance revenue but also as a social and moral duty towards women, they launched a new service called Shuttle in Dhaka in July 2018 with two microbuses. This service was designed for women in the workforce and students on their way to or returning from university.

An early-stage startup needed much capital to get off the ground. ROBI's r-Ventures initiative[11] provided Shuttle with a significant amount of funding.

In 2020, the Bangladeshi branch of the Chartered Institute of Logistics and Transport (CILT) nominated Riasat Chowdhury (Riasat), co-founder and CEO of Shuttle, for the Young Achiever Award. The nomination was a recognition of the important initiative taken by Riasat in the country's transport system – to provide safe and comfortable transportation services for women.

The Arrival of Shuttle: A Safe Haven for Women on Road

The people of the country, especially the people of Dhaka, Chittagong, and Sylhet, were well acquainted with the app-based communication system due to many applications like Uber or Pathao.[12]

Shuttle was launched on similar lines, as an app-based pickup and drop service to provide safe, secure, and comfortable transportation to women. Each Shuttle vehicle could transport ten passengers. The passenger needed to book a journey through the company's website or an app compatible with the iPhone and Android operating systems to board the Shuttle and register. The users could also register by directly calling the customer helpline. The passenger had to book a ride at least one hour before the journey. The booking could also be done a day in advance. Each microbus had a trip manager with the driver, who informed passengers by phone 15 minutes before the start of the ride. Shuttle verified the background of the trip managers and made them accountable. Shah Sufian Mahmud Chowdhury, co-founder and CTO of Shuttle, said:

> We take utmost care in hiring drivers and trip managers. At the end of the preliminary selection, each employee is given the final appointment after performing the training duties. This is our step to ensure the quality of service and customer satisfaction.

The Shuttle microbuses were modern; they were air-conditioned and had comfortable seats. Shuttle had 18 microbuses covering six routes in Dhaka.[13] The first ride started at 6:40 in the morning and continued up to 7:30 in the evening.

A Shuttle service cost much less than CNG autorickshaws or any other ride-sharing. New passengers got a chance to enjoy three to six rides for free. After the free rides, passengers needed to buy a ticket at a fixed fare. There were two types of tickets – single and bundle. Bundle tickets provided ten ride opportunities; there were also special discounts. Customers were required to pay a fixed fare based on the route. For example, a single ticket from Bashundhara to Mirpur was US$1.16, while a bundle ticket was US$10.44. About 1,000 women opted for the company's transport services daily, especially in Dhaka City. Jawad Jahangir, co-founder and COO of Shuttle, said, 'We have a Facebook community of 7,000 female passengers. We, the co-founders, are the admins of this group. We take every word of the members seriously and try to resolve any issues as soon as possible' (see Figure 13.1 for the features of the Shuttle). He added:

> Everyone in this country is concerned about women's safety. This service of the Shuttle is from that thought. The trip managers are the Shuttle's staff. After checking and

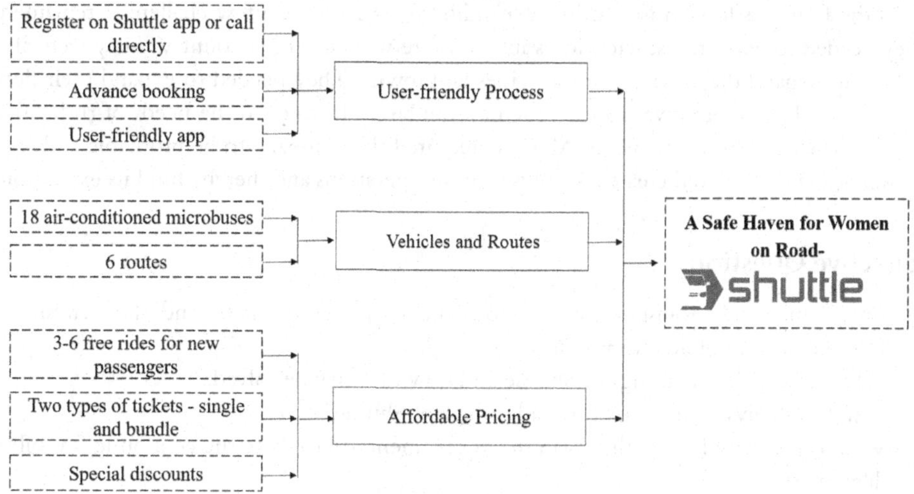

FIGURE 13.1 Features of Shuttle.

Source: Compiled by the authors.

sorting, the car and driver are hired. Before the start of the trip, drivers are also given training on various topics including behaviour.[14]

Many travellers claimed that Shuttle offered them three advantages. It provided safety and comfortable and hassle-free travel. It also offered a variety of automobiles to its customers, such as Hiace, Noahs, Sedans, and Coasters. Businesses that wanted to provide transport facilities to their employees also used the Shuttle service.

Looking Ahead

Shuttle's popularity grew over the years, and several women used the service for hassle-free, safe travel. Many customers said they were pleased with its services and its quality. According to Tasnia Islam Risa, a student, 'The ways in which Shuttle gives customers routes and delivers their services is very convenient for people. This is because Shuttle caters to the needs of its customers.'[15]

Shuttle showed rapid growth, and its services also spread quickly. Riasat said, 'Currently, we have about 1,000 rides daily on six routes. Every month we are launching the service on new routes. We are working to ensure that women in Bangladesh do not have to worry about safety when traveling.'[16]

The founders were looking at increasing the reach of the service by operating on additional routes. They were also looking to make travel safer and more convenient for women in Dhaka. They planned to introduce technology to share the passengers' whereabouts with the family members so that the members could see it through the app. There were also plans to introduce a system to monitor the vehicles and passengers directly through CCTV cameras in the future.

In 2020, the Bangladeshi branch of the Chartered Institute of Logistics and Transport (CILT) nominated Riasat for the Young Achiever Award. The nomination was a recognition of the important initiative taken by Riasat in the country's transport system to provide safe and comfortable transportation services for women,

As the founders looked forward to expanding their services, a few challenges remained. They needed to make the service accessible to more women in the country. They were also looking to expand the service to other cities and towns. They needed to expand their fleet as well to include alternatives to cars, such as minibuses, to cater to the needs of rush-hour commuters to and from the office. All these required the company to be profitable and self-sustaining so that it would create a surplus from its operations and thereby fund its expansion.

Reflective Questions

1. Are women-only transportation options the proper solution to end the harassment women face in public transportation?
2. What are the shortcomings of Shuttle and how can they be solved?
3. Critically analyse the competitive advantage of Shuttle.
4. What can stakeholders, other than the government, do to solve the economic feasibility dilemma?

Activities

1. Record instances of gender discrimination in your neighbourhood and compare them with what happens in a different area. Analyse the possible reasons for the differences and present your findings in class.
2. Prepare a note on what actions you would like to take as a citizen to prevent acts of discrimination in society.
3. Form three member teams and design an awareness campaign on the problem of gender bias and discrimination.

Notes

1 'Labor Force, Total – Bangladesh', https://data.worldbank.org/indicator/SL.TLF.TOTL.IN?locations=BD.
2 ActionAid is an international non-governmental organization that works against poverty and injustice.
3 BRAC is an international development organization based in Bangladesh.
4 Manikganj is a district in Central Bangladesh.
5 Sonargaon is a city in Central Bangladesh.
6 Barisal is a city in South-Central Bangladesh.
7 Mymensingh is a city North of Dhaka.
8 'Mymensingh Girl Raped on Bus, Driver Held', *The Daily Star*, January 6, 2016, www.thedailystar.net/country/mymensingh-girl-raped-bus-driver-held-197917.
9 Mobility justice examines whether the transportation system is safe, comfortable, and environmentally sustainable for everybody (Sheller, 2018).
10 S Bishwas, 'Only the Name of BRTC, Invisible Dolonchapa', *KalerKantho*, March 8, 2021, www.kalerkantho.com/print-edition/first-page/2021/03/08/1011885.
11 Robi's r-Ventures is a flagship digital entrepreneurship program which provides funding for startups.
12 Pathao offers motorbike taxis and logistics services in Bangladesh.
13 The routes were from Uttara to Bashundhara, from Mirpur to Bashundhara, from Dhanmondi to Bashundhara, from Mohammadpur to Bashundhara, from Dhanmondi to Gulshan, and from Mirpur to Mohammadpur via Gulshan and Rampura.
14 Shuttle Brings Safe, 'Comfortable Transportation for City Women', *New Age*, February 27, 2019, www.newagebd.net/article/65964/shuttle-brings-safe-comfortable-transportation-for-city-women.

15 Nafiz Ahmed, 'An Overview of Shuttle: A Promising Mass Transit Startup in Bangladesh', *UNB News*, June 8, 2021, www.unb.com.bd/m/category/Business/an-overview-of-shuttle-a-promising-mass-transit-startup-in-bangladesh/73182.

16 Shuttle Brings Safe, 'Comfortable Transportation for City Women', *New Age*, February 27, 2019, www.newagebd.net/article/65964/shuttle-brings-safe-comfortable-transportation-for-city-women.

Additional References and Supplemental Readings

'94% Women Victims of Sexual Harassment in Public Transport', *BRAC*, March 25, 2018, www.brac.net/latest-news/item/1142-94-women-victims-of-sexual-harassment-in-public-transport.

Afrin, S., 'Shuttle Facilitates Women's Transportation', *Prothom Alo*, October 12, 2019, www.prothomalo.com/life

Ahmed, M., 'The Number of Women in the Workforce is Increasing', *Prothom Alo*, October 18, 2019.

Babu, T., 'How Safe Are Women in Night Public Transport in Bangladesh?' *BBC News*, February 12, 2018, www.bbc.com/bengali/news-43032401

'CILT Nominates Shuttle's CEO for International Young Achiever Award', *Robi*, February 6, 2019, www.robi.com.bd/bn/corporate/media-room/press-release/chartered-institute-of-logistics-and-transport-nominates-shuttles-ceo-for-international-young-achiever-award.

Gardner, C., 'Safe Conduct: Women, Crime, and Self in Public Places', *Semantic Scholar*, August 1, 1990.

Gardner, N., Cui, J., & Coiacetto, E., 'Harassment on Public Transport and Its Impacts on Women's Travel Behavior', *Australian Planner*, *54*(1) (2017), 8–15.

Gekoski, A., Gray, J. M., Adler, J. R., & Horvath, M. A., 'The Prevalence and Nature of Sexual Harassment and Assault Against Women and Girls on Public Transport: An International Review', *Journal of Criminological Research Policy and Practice, 3*(1) (2017), 3–16.

Hossain, M., 'Women's Bus: The Number of Passengers is Less', *Prothom Alo*, September 7, 2015.

Mahmud, A., 'Violence against Women in Public Transport', *The Daily Inqilab*, November 7, 2019, www.dailyinqilab.com/article/246362e.

Painter, K., 'Different Worlds: The Spatial, Temporal and Social Dimensions of Female Victimization', in D. J. Evans, N. R. Fyfe, & D. T. Herbert (eds.), *Crime, Policing and Place* (pp. 164–195), Routledge: London, 1992.

Sheller, M., 'Theorising Mobility Justice', *Tempo Social, 30*(2) (2018), 17–34.

PART X
Economic Development

14

FARM SECTOR REFORMS IN INDIA

A Tough Road Ahead for the Government

G.V. Muralidhara

Synopsis

Indian agricultural sector was characterized by small holdings and water-intensive farming. The sector provided employment to more than 40% of the country's population but contributed only 20% to the GDP.

Given the sensitive nature of the sector, the successive governments had avoided implementing large-scale reforms in the sector. The sector was supported through subsidized fertilizers and electricity as well as minimum support prices for the produce.

In September 2020, the government implemented three bills aimed at deregulating the farm sector and allowing private players to take up contract farming. It aimed to provide the farmers access to private markets which was not available earlier. The farmers apprehended that these reforms would expose them to the vagaries of the free market and make them poorer. The protracted agitation of farmers against the farm laws drew national as well as worldwide attention. After an initial reluctance to yield to the farmers' demands, the government announced withdrawal of the farm laws in November 2021. The entire episode brought into focus the government's approach in pushing an important reform without building a broad consensus among stakeholders.

On November 19, 2021, in his broadcast to the nation, India's Prime Minister Narendra Modi (Modi), announced that the government had decided to repeal the three farm bills that the government had earlier implemented.[1] The farmers from Punjab and Haryana were protesting in Delhi from November 2020, demanding a repeal of the three bills the government had passed in the parliament in September 2020.

Through these bills, the government aimed at providing farmers access to private markets instead of restricting them to the Agricultural Market Committee (APMC) Mandis,[2]

DOI: 10.4324/9781003261155-25

facilitating contract farming and deregulating the production, storage, movement, and sale of several primary food produce.[3] The government had maintained that the laws would increase the farmers' income, and Modi had called the reforms a watershed moment for Indian agriculture. On the other hand, the farmers apprehended that these laws would expose them to the vagaries of the free market and make them poorer.[4]

Small and fragmented holdings dominated India's agricultural sector. Agriculture was not a lucrative activity in the country. Though the sector employed more than 40% of the country's population, its contribution to the GDP was only around 20% (see Figures 14.1–14.3).

Some analysts opined that the move to repeal the farm bills by Modi was motivated by the upcoming elections in Uttar Pradesh, the most populous state in India.[5] Other analysts cautioned the government to push reforms and not yield to further unreasonable farmers' demands.[6] Some experts felt that the repeal of the farm laws would be a setback for India's economic reforms and would discourage political parties from attempting agriculture reforms in the near term.[7]

Ashish Vaidya, managing director and head of emerging markets, DBS Bank, opined that there would be a negative impact on global investors' sentiment towards India due to the repeal of farm laws.[8] In the meantime, the farmers' union announced that they would not be calling off the agitation and demanded acceptance of other demands, including the legalization of the minimum support price.[9],[10]

The government was in a tight spot and had to figure out a way to appease the farmers and keep the reforms agenda moving ahead. Modi had to now find a way to balance the need to progress on the reforms agenda in the farm sector taking all the stakeholders along.

Agriculture Sector in India

Agriculture was the largest source of livelihood in the country. The sector predominantly consisted of small and marginal farmers. India was one of the largest producers of many food grains globally. However, the sector's contribution to the country's GDP had declined steadily

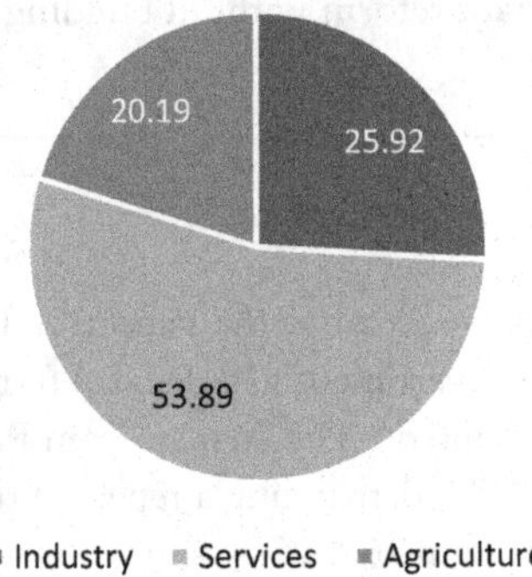

FIGURE 14.1 India: sectoral contribution to GDP.

Source: https://statisticstimes.com/economy/country/india-gdp-sectorwise.php

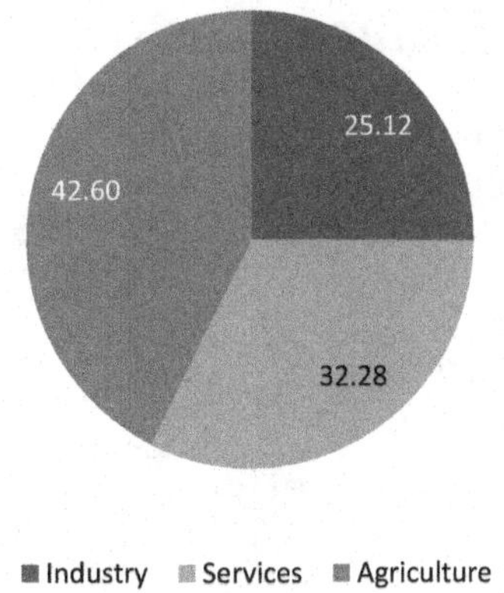

FIGURE 14.2 Sector-wise distribution of workforce.

Source: https://statista.com/statistics/271320/distribution-of-the-worksforce-across-economic-sectors-in-india/

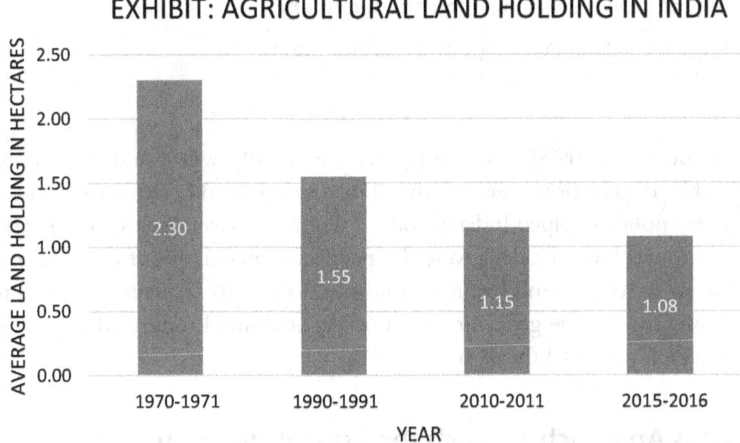

FIGURE 14.3 Agricultural land holding in India.

Source: Gulati, A., Juneja, R., "Transforming Indian Agriculture" In: Chand, R., Joshi, P., Khadka, S. (eds) Indian Agriculture Towards 2030. India Studies in Business and Economics. Springer, Singapore.

over the years (see Figure 14.4). The sector was labour-intensive with low levels of mechanization. The production was cereal-centric and resource-intensive, leading to questions of sustainability.[11]

Green Revolution

India's green revolution, which started in the 1960s, aimed to get the country out of the food-deficit status. The government provided subsidies for fertilizers and electricity and

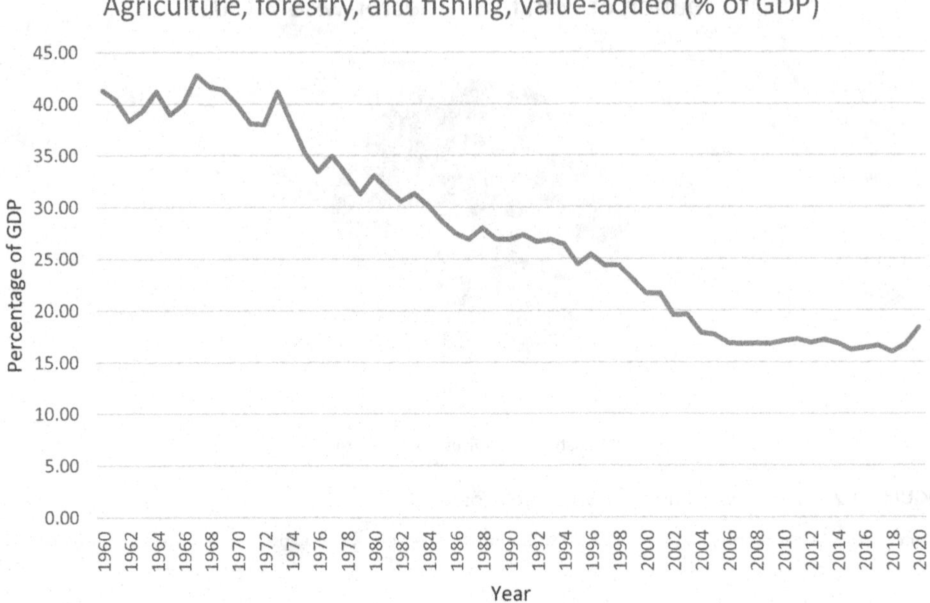

FIGURE 14.4 Value added: agriculture, forestry, and fishing.

Source: 'World Development Indicators,' https://data.worldbank.org/indicator/

minimum support prices (MSP) for the produce, especially wheat and rice. It also implemented the public distribution system to distribute essential food grains at subsidized rates to the poor.[12] These policies helped India become a wheat and rice surplus nation. The states of Punjab, Haryana, and Uttar Pradesh were the primary beneficiaries of the MSP regime and contributed majorly to the production of wheat and rice. To facilitate the procurement of food grains from farmers, the government set up Agricultural Produce Marketing Committee (APMC), which procured through Mandis.[13]

Government's Approach Towards the Agriculture Sector

The green revolution during the 1960s put Indian agriculture on a growth trajectory and helped the country achieve self-sufficiency and food security. However, the 1980s saw a decline in productivity in agriculture due to a reduction in public investment in irrigation projects. The provision of subsidized inputs did not help in increasing productivity. There were no policy interventions in agriculture when the country went through economic reforms during the 1990s. The significant increases in MSP during the latter part of the 1990s made the conditions relatively favourable for the farmers. However, fragmentation of holdings, labour, and water-intensive farming created challenges.

During the 2000s, the government continued to support agriculture through subsidies, higher MSP, and investments in irrigation projects. Successive governments avoided initiating significant reforms in the farm sector. They went about providing remedies like loan waivers in the light of the incidence of farmer suicides due to their indebtedness.[14] The manufacturing sector failed to create employment for the movement of people away from the farm sector. The agriculture sector continued to employ a significant portion of the population.[15] Agriculture being a state subject created additional challenges for implementing any reforms in the sector.

Reforms in the Agriculture Sector

The federal structure of the Indian Constitution provided the states with primary responsibility for many aspects related to agriculture. The central government's role was to provide a direction to the policy and provide funds to the states to implement policies. Because of this arrangement, all the states did not uniformly implement the schemes initiated by the central government. Also, multiple ministries and departments had a say on the matters of agriculture sector.

The policies related to agriculture in the country focused mainly on managing the prices of agricultural products and the distribution channels, providing inputs for farming at subsidized rates, and providing food grains at subsidized rates to specific groups of the population. In addition, it focused on research and extension services to the farming community and formulating policies to regulate border transactions of food grains. Two important aspects that governed the agricultural sector in India were the Essential Commodities Act (ECA) and the Agriculture Produce Marketing Committee Act (APMC Act). The APMC Act prevented private players from setting up wholesale markets and empowered only the state governments to set up and manage agriculture markets. Though there had been moves to relax these restrictions and allow private players through acts like Model Agricultural Produce and Livestock Marketing Act 2017, the implementation had not been uniform across states. There were differences between the prices set by the government under the minimum support price mechanism and international reference prices.[16] There were no significant changes in policies relating to the provision of subsidized farm inputs like fertilizers, seeds, electricity, surface water, and the tax concessions available on agricultural income. The government followed a policy of import tariffs and export restrictions consistently with minor tweaks during some periods.[17]

In June 2020, the government promulgated three ordinances which came to be known as Farm laws. Three bills introduced and passed by the parliament in September 2020 replaced these. The three bills were – Farmers Produce Trade and Commerce (Promotion and Facilitation) Bill, 2020; Farmers (Empowerment and Protection) Agreement on Price Assurance and Farm Services Bill, 2020; and Essential Commodities (Amendment) Bill, 2020.[18] These bills aimed to provide the farmers access to private markets to sell their produce, deregulating the production, storage, movement, and sale of farm produce and allowing contract farming (see Table 14.1).

Farmers' Agitation

As soon as the Indian Parliament passed the bills on September 20, 2020, farmers in the primary states producing rice and wheat started protesting against these on September 24, 2020. The protests spread gradually to other parts of the country and even to places like London and Melbourne. The talks between the farmers' representatives and the government did not solve this. On January 12, 2021, the Supreme Court of India ordered a stay on the implementation

TABLE 14.1 Farm Bills: Important Features

The Farmers' Produce Trade and Commerce (Promotion and Facilitation) Act, 2020, was an act to provide for the creation of an ecosystem where the farmers and traders had the freedom of choice relating to sale and purchase of farmers' produce. This was aimed at facilitating remunerative prices through competitive alternative trading channels promoting efficient, transparent, and barrier-free inter-state and intra-state trade and commerce of farmers' produce outside the physical premises of markets notified under various state agricultural market legislations. It was also aimed at providing a facilitating framework for electronic trading.
The Farmers' (Empowerment and Protection) Agreement on Price Assurance and Farm Services Act, 2020, was an act to provide for a national framework on framing agreements that protected and empowered farmers to engage with agri-business firms, processors, wholesalers, exporters, or large retailers for farm services and sale of future farming produce at a mutually agreed price framework in a fair and transparent manner
The essential Commodities (Amendment) Act, 2020, amended the Essential Commodities Act, 1955, to bring the purview of the regulation to only extraordinary circumstances which may include war, famine, extraordinary price rise, and natural calamity of grave nature and provided for imposing a stock limit only in case of 100% increase in the retail price of horticultural produce or 50% increase in the retail price of non-perishable agricultural foodstuffs. The regulation of stock limit did not apply to a processor or value chain participant of any agricultural produce under specified conditions.

Source: The Gazette of India notification No. CG-DL-E-27092020–222039 dated September 27, 2020; The Gazette of India notification No. CG-DL-E-27092020–222040 dated September 27, 2020; The Gazette of India notification No. CG-DL-E-27092020–222038 dated September 27, 2020.

of these laws. However, farmers continued their protest, demanding a total withdrawal of the bills.[19] Thousands of farmers camped on the Delhi border for over a year braving severe weather and away from their farms. On November 19, 2021, the prime minister announced that the government would repeal the laws. In his address to the nation, he said that the government did not communicate well to the farmers though the legislations were for the benefit of the farmers.

The Road Ahead

Experts opined that the government should follow a more consultative and participative approach to implement any reforms in the agriculture sector.[20] The Agri-tech players were not happy as they could not harness scale economies because of the repeal of farm laws. The government had to figure out ways to bring out agricultural reforms, improve productivity, enable the use of technology, and enhance farmers' income.[21] It was to be seen how Modi will navigate this challenge and push the government's progressive agenda.

Reflective Questions

1. Though the Indian Government's action to implement reforms in the farm sector was well intentioned, it failed in gaining the acceptance of farmers. What do you think were the main reasons for this?

2. If you were the head of a task force entrusted with the responsibility of implementing the reforms, how would you go about implementing it?
3. Discuss the challenges faced by the government in bringing about major reforms in a sector like agriculture in a democracy. Can you cite an example of a country that has been successful in implementing major reforms? How did they manage the process?

Activities

1. Create teams of two students – one team representing the government and the other team representing the farmers. Carry out negotiations to find a solution.
2. Create small teams of two to three students and identify a prioritized list of reforms required in the agriculture sector in India.

Notes

1 'Cabinet Approves Bill to Repeal Three Farm Laws; Bill to Be Tabled in Parliament in Winter Session', November 24, 2021, accessed November 25, 2021, https://economictimes.indiatimes.com/policy/union-cabinet-approves-farm-laws-repeal-bill-sources.
2 Mandi was a local wholesale market facilitating the sale of farm produce.
3 Priscilla Debraj, 'Hindu Explains – Who Gains and Who Loses from the Farm Bills', September 27, 2020, accessed November 25, 2021, https://thehindu.com/news/national/the-hindu-explains-who-gains-and-who-loses-from-the-farm-bills.
4 'Bharat Bandh: India Farmers Strike to Press for Repeal of Laws', September 27, 2021, accessed November 25, 2021, https://bbc.om/news/world-asia-india-54233080.
5 Capt. CR Gopinath, 'Modi: Statesman or Pretender', *Deccan Herald*, November 24, 2021.
6 'Draw a Red Line', *The Times of India*, November 22, 2021.
7 Gautam Chikermane, 'Modi's U-Turn on Farm Laws: A Setback in the History of India's Economic Reforms', November 19, 2021, accessed November 24, 2021, https://orfonline.org/expert-speak/modis-u-turn-on-farm-laws/.
8 'Repeal of Farm Laws May Hurt Rupee, Debt Markets', *The Economic Times*, November 22, 2021.
9 'Protests to Continue Till Govt Gives Legal Guarantee on MSP, Says SKM', *The Economic Times*, November 22, 2021.
10 Minimum Support Price (MSP) was a minimum price guarantee that the government provided to farmers through a procurement mechanism. This acted as a safety for farmers against fluctuations in prices.
11 'India at a Glance', https://fao.org/india/fao-in-india/india-at-a glance/en/.
12 Marshall M Boulton, 'The Paradox of India's Green Revolution', accessed November 30, 2021, https://thehindubusinessline.com/opinion/the-paradox-of-india's-green-revolution/.
13 Nives Dolsak and Aseem Prakash, 'The Green Revolution Is in Trouble: Here's Why Indian Farmers Are Protesting', accessed November 30, 2021, https://forbes.com/sites/prakashdolsak/2020/12/20.
14 Most of the farmers had a hand to mouth existence because of small holdings. They did not generate much surplus in each cycle of cropping. They ended up taking loans at the beginning of every farming season. When the crops failed due to bad weather or drought, they ended up with a debt.
15 Seema Bathla and Siraj Hussain, 'Indian Agriculture Towards 2030-Structural Reforms and Governance', accessed December 1, 2021, https://fao.org/. . ./FAO-countries/India/.
16 These are prices determined with prices in foreign markets as benchmark.
17 'Review of Agriculture Policies of India', Trade and Agriculture Directorate Committee for Agriculture, OECD, July 4, 2018.
18 https://indianexpress.com/article/india/india/pm-modi-repeals-farm-bills-a-timeline-of-events-that-followed-since-their-enactment-7630402/, November 20, 2021, accessed December 22, 2021.

19 www.reuters.com/markets/commodities/indian-farmers-protests-against-agricultural-laws-2021-11-19/, accessed December 23, 2021.

20 'UN Expert Welcomes India Plan to Repeal Farm Laws That Sparked Deadly Protests', accessed December 23, 2021, news.un.org/en/story/2021/11/1106632.

21 Manasvini Kaushik, 'Farm Laws Repeal: What Lies Ahead', accessed December 23, 2021, Forbesindia.com/article/special/farm-laws-repeal-what-lies-ahead/71657/1.

15

SRI LANKA IN CRISIS

A Difficult Road Ahead?

G.V. Muralidhara

Synopsis

During April 2022, the Sri Lankan government took the unprecedented step of announcing that it would default on its foreign debt in light of the acute economic crisis the country faced. This was a huge setback for a once prosperous island nation in the Indian Ocean. The country had a population of 21.92 million and a GDP of US$80.68 billion in 2020. The country depended on tourism and export of tea which were affected by the COVID-19 pandemic and the ill-advised ban on chemical fertilizers by the government, respectively. The government also took a populist measure of cutting down taxes in 2019 which resulted in a fall in revenue. The country had resorted to external debts to balance its fiscal deficits on a regular basis and the sudden fall in export earnings resulted in a drastic fall in the country's forex reserves. As the country faced severe shortage of fuel and other essential goods and spiralling inflation, citizens took to the streets and went on mass protests against the government. The country faced the daunting task of finding ways to come out of the economic crisis and bringing back a semblance of normalcy to the economy.

Introduction

On June 22, 2022, Ranil Wickremesinghe (Wickremesinghe), the Prime Minister of Sri Lanka, stated in the country's parliament that the country's economy had collapsed and warned that the country would fall to a rock bottom.[1] Earlier on June 7, 2022, he had appealed to the country's citizens to be united and patient and avoid hoarding of scarce commodities like fuel and gas. He hoped that after three weeks the country would find a way out of the immediate crisis and make food and fuel available to the citizens without disruptions.[2] Wickremesinghe had taken over as the Prime Minister on May 12, 2022, after Mahinda

DOI: 10.4324/9781003261155-26

Rajapaksa (Mahinda), the then Prime Minister, resigned from the post on May 9, 2022, after violent anti-government protests by citizens over the failure of the government to arrest the worsening economic crisis the country was going through.[3]

Sri Lanka, an island nation in the Indian Ocean, had India as its immediate neighbour separated from it by the Palk Strait. It had a population of 21.92 million and a GDP of US$80.68 billion in 2020.[4] Its economy depended mainly on export of primary commodities and tourism. The country depended on import of essential food items as well as fuel, fertilizers, and non-agricultural consumer goods. After a long civil war from 1983 to 2009, the economy had a period of growth from 2009 to 2012. However, the economy started declining after 2012 as a result of falling commodity prices. A series of bomb blasts in 2019 in Colombo, the capital, resulted in a decline in tourist arrivals. Also, the new government that came to power in November 2019 announced major tax cuts which resulted in a sharp decline in tax revenues. The tax cut resulted in a loss of more than 2% of GDP and in addition caused suspension of the existing International Monetary Fund (IMF) programme.[5,6] The COVID-19[7] pandemic further exacerbated the situation affecting tourist arrivals and commodity exports. The fiscal deficit[8] increased to more than 10% in 2020 and 2021 combined with a rise in the ratio of public debt to GDP to 119% in 2021.[9,10] At the same time, there was also pressure on foreign exchange.

In April 2021, the government announced that the import of all fertilizers would be banned from May 2021 with the intention of moving to total organic farming. This severely impacted the agricultural production in 2021–2022. Though the organic farming policy was withdrawn in November 2021, the damage it had caused to the economy was significant. With the continued shrinking of the economy, drastic fall in its foreign exchange reserves and the spiralling of commodity prices internationally due to Ukraine war,[11] there were severe shortages of essential goods leading to mass protests by the citizens.

On April 12, 2022, the government announced that it would default on its foreign debt in light of the worst economic crisis the country faced post-independence.[12] On April 13, 2022, the World Bank stated that Sri Lanka's economic outlook was extremely uncertain due to the fiscal and external imbalances. It further stated that the country had to reduce fiscal deficits through strengthening of resource mobilization and also find feasible options to ensure sustainability of debt.[13] In 2019, The Asian Development Bank had described Sri Lanka's economy as 'a tale of two deficits.' The nation had a trade deficit as it imported more than it exported and had a budget deficit as it spent more than its revenue on a regular basis.

As the worsening economic situation tested the patience of its citizens who struggled to secure essential goods amid spiralling prices, the world was watching how the country would pull itself out of the crisis, get back to normalcy, and on a path to recovery and growth.[14]

Sri Lanka: Roots of the Economic Problems

At the time of its independence in 1948,[15] Sri Lanka inherited an economy characterized by export dependency and dominated by export of three commodities – tea, rubber, and coconut. The country continued on this path with an open policy framework that was endorsed by the World Bank. During the initial years, this strategy worked for the country due to the commodity boom on account of the Korean war.[16] However, with the end of the war, exports grew slowly and imports remained high. This led to the import controls by the government from 1959 to 1976. The widening of the current account deficit necessitated availing assistance from the IMF and consequently moving towards a liberal economic order that was market friendly.[17]

Economic Reforms 1977–1983

In 1977, the government launched an economic reform program which consisted of removal of quantitative restrictions on imports and exports, a large devaluation of the currency, liberalization of exchange restrictions, and a shift to a managed float of the exchange rate.[18] This led to a spurt in the inflow of foreign aid. IMF extended lending of 93 million, 260 million, and 50 million SDRs[19] in 1977, 1979, and 1983, respectively.[20] Critiques pointed out that the period post-liberalization was characterized by rising inequality, a fall in social expenditure, and a fall in public expenditure on health and food subsidy.[21]

The Debt Dependency

The current account deficit[22] of Sri Lanka was at an average of around 1.2% of GDP during the period 2010–2019.[23] The country financed its current account deficits with a continuous flow of foreign borrowing. The external debt which was at US$1.1 billion in 1977 rose to US$9.25 billion in 2000 and to US$56.34 billion in 2020 (see Figure 15.1). In 2020,

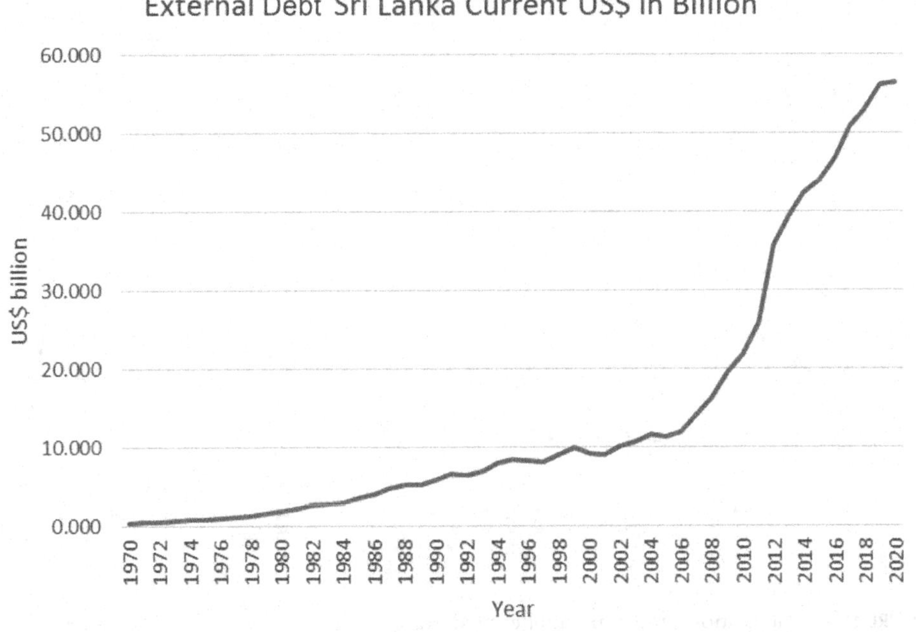

FIGURE 15.1 External debt of Sri Lanka.

Source: IMF.

sovereign bonds[24] constituted 36.4% of Sri Lanka's external debt, Asian Development Bank[25] at 14.3%, Japan at 10.9%, and China at 10.8% were other major contributors. The country was due to pay US$7 billion of the foreign debt in 2022 out of the US$25 billion that was due by 2026. At the beginning of May 2022, the usable foreign reserves of the country had gone down to less than US$50 million.[26]

With a fall in foreign exchange reserves by 70% between the beginning of January 2020 and March 2022, the Sri Lankan Rupee depreciated sharply. Though the government tried to hold the currency up, it had to allow the currency to float resulting in the Sri Lankan Rupee settling at Rs.200 rupees to a dollar by April 2021 and 300 rupees to a dollar by end March 2022.[27]

The Civil War

Sri Lanka went through a long civil war from 1983 to 2009 which left its share of impact on the economy. It was a conflict between Liberation Tigers of Tamil Eelam (LTTE), an insurgent group, and the Sri Lankan government dominated by the Sinhalese. The conflict had its origins in the provision of better development opportunities for the Tamil population during the British rule prior to 1948 and the suppression of Tamils by the majority Sinhalese post-independence. LTTE fought for a separate country for Tamils who were geographically concentrated in the northern and eastern parts of the country.[28] The country saw a sharp increase in defence expenditure during this period. The war also affected the international tourist arrivals (see Figure 15.2). The country's economy did not make much progress during this period as the contribution of agriculture to the GDP dropped from 28% to 7.7% and the

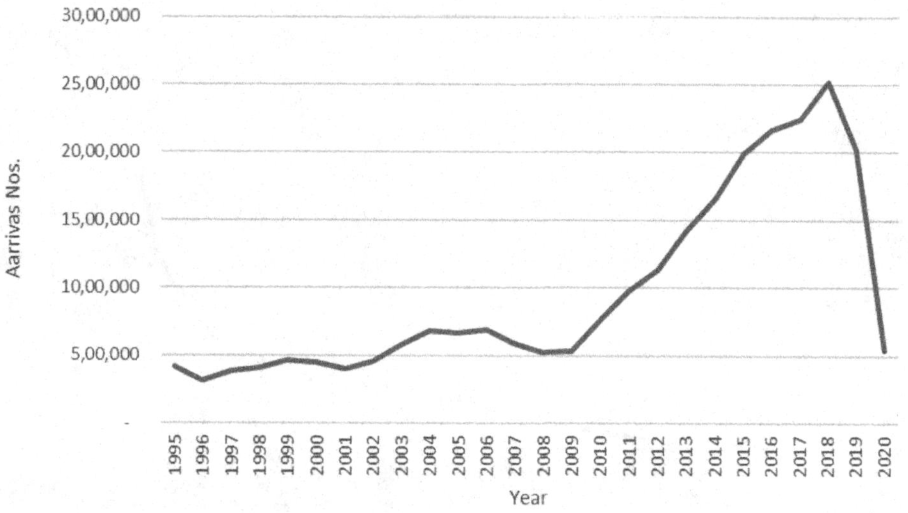

FIGURE 15.2 International tourism: number of arrivals.

Source: IMF.

contribution of the industry remained between 17% and 19%. The contribution of services increased from 54% to 73%.[29]

The Pandemic

COVID-19 pandemic which impacted most of the countries adversely impacted Sri Lanka as well. It affected the agricultural, industrial, and tourism sectors and resulted in a growth rate of −3.6% in Sri Lanka's GDP (at market prices based on constant local currency).[30] The pandemic also adversely impacted the foreign exchange remittance into the country. It affected the livelihoods of a large section of the population. Exports of goods and services as a percentage of GDP went down from 23.1% in 2019 to 16.6% in 2020. The pandemic resulted in the fiscal deficit exceeding 10% in 2020 and 2021 and also a rise in public debt to GDP ratio to 119% in 2021.[31]

Switch to Organic Farming

Based on the advice of environmentalists, in 2019 the President of Sri Lanka announced a vision for the country to completely transition to organic farming. Faced with a foreign exchange crisis, in April 2021, the government completely banned the import of fertilizers and agrochemicals. Though the intention was to promote healthy and sustainable farming, the impact was severe. Food production went down with 33% of agricultural land being left unused. The tea industry incurred substantial losses to the tune of US$425 million, impacting the foreign exchange earnings. Experts criticized the government for taking this hasty step without considering the implications.[32]

Spiralling Inflation and Shortage of Commodities

In June 2022, Wickremesinghe informed the parliament that the country would need $3.3 billion for fuel imports, $900 million for food, $250 million for cooking gas, and $600 million for fertilizer during the remaining part of the year. The country was renegotiating a loan of $3 billion from the IMF. The country had utilized loans from the IMF several times in the past and all these had come with conditionalities. In 2016, the country had approached IMF for a 16th loan amounting to $1.5 billion for the period 2016–2019. It was also renegotiating a yuan-denominated swap with China to tide over the crisis.[33] India had extended to Sri Lanka around $3 billion through various routes to enable the country manage the crisis. This included currency swaps, credit lines for supply of fuel, and assistance for deferment of loans of $900 million under the Asian Clearing Union.[34] In addition, the government of Tamil Nadu, a southern state of India, provided assistance in the form of consignments of rice, milk powder, and drugs.[35] The country witnessed a steep rise in inflation, reaching 39.1% with food inflation touching 57.4% and inflation of non-food items at 30.6% in May 2022[36] (see Figure 15.3). As citizens struggled to make ends meet, they faced long queues at gas stations. Schools and government offices were closed due to a severe fuel shortage. There were long power shutdowns because of non-availability of fuel.[37] Earlier the authorities had cancelled school exams because of paper shortage.[38] Hospitals were postponing treatments because of shortage of medicines. The government was applying for aid from SAARC-operated[39] food bank to meet the food shortage.[40]

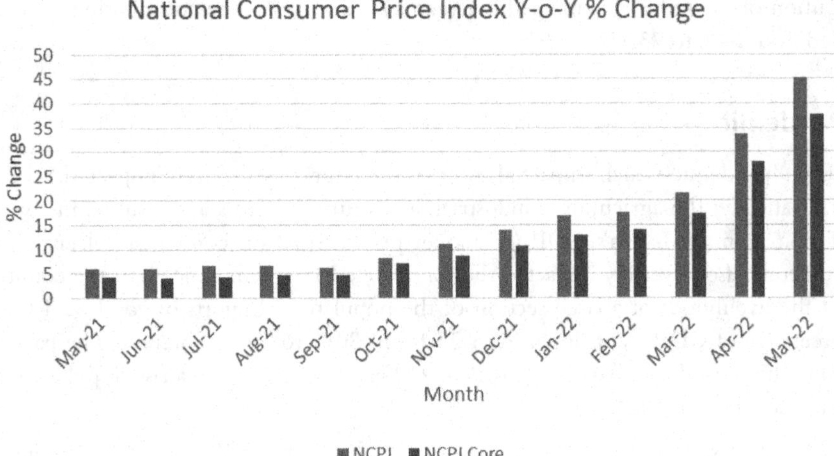

FIGURE 15.3 National consumer price index.

Source: Central Bank of Sri Lanka.

The Road Ahead

The challenges in front of the Sri Lankan government were huge. The immediate task was to restore normalcy by securing sufficient aid to sail through the crisis and ensure regular supply of essential commodities. Government finances needed to be straightened up by taking some tough measures on the tax front which could be unpopular. The economy required a kick start with steps to make available adequate supplies. Export-oriented industries in the country were dependent upon imported inputs. Long-term measures were necessary to bring down the country's dependence on debt. Unless the general conditions in the country improved, there was no possibility of a revival of the tourism industry.

The world was watching with concern how Sri Lanka, a once prosperous nation, would navigate itself out of the crisis and get back on a growth path. The journey towards days of growth and prosperity looked quite long. Wickremesinghe had the toughest job in his political career ahead. Will he be able to lead Sri Lanka out of the crisis?

Reflective Questions

1. To what extent do you think were the developments in Sri Lanka leading to the economic crisis a result of unforeseen events like the pandemic and a result of bad policies and decisions?
2. If you were the finance minister of the country, what steps would you have taken to prevent the rapid deterioration that the country faced causing hardships to the citizens?
3. If you were the governor of the central bank of the country, what steps will you take to prevent a forex crisis like the one in 2022?

Activities

1. You are working in the Prime Minister's office of Sri Lanka. You have been asked to prepare the content for the Prime Minister's address to the nation explaining the situation the country was facing, and what was being done by the government to alleviate the problems and bring normalcy in the economy.
2. Form teams of three students each and prepare a position paper on the economic implications of the initiative to implement organic farming in the country.

Notes

1 Sri Lanka's Prime Minister says, economy has collapsed, *The Guardian*, June 22, 2022.
2 https://frontiline.thehindu.com/dispatches/sri-lanka-pm-ranil-wikremsinghe-requests-patience-as-un-calls-for-relief-funds/article65503448.ece.
3 https://frontiline.thehindu.com/world-affairs/Sri-lanka-crisis-gotabaya-rajapaksa-the making-and-unmaking-of-a-president/article38491294.ece.
4 Databank.worldbank.org.
5 The IMF's $1.5 billion lending to Sri Lanka included a reduction of the budget deficit to 3.5% of the GDP in 2020, which was to be achieved through increase of taxes, cut down in welfare programs, and restructuring of the economy.
6 Akhil Bery, 'The Crisis in Sri Lanka', *Atlantic Council*, June 3, 2022.
7 During 2020 and 2021, the world was affected by the COVID-19 pandemic which forced many countries impose lockdowns resulting in limited economic activity. This affected the economic growth of most countries.
8 Fiscal deficit is the gap between the total revenue of the government and the total expenditure. This has to be balanced by borrowings by the government.
9 P Ramakumar, 'Roots of Sri Lanka's Economic Crisis', *Frontline*, April 22, 2022.
10 This ratio indicated how many years the government would need to repay its debt if it used its GDP for repayment. A higher debt to GDP ratio signalled a possibility of a default.
11 In early 2022, the war between Ukraine and Russia resulted in large-scale disruptions in the flow of commodities globally and also resulted in a steep increase in oil prices.
12 bbc.com/news/business-61076481.
13 'Sri Lanka Faces Unsustainable Debt and Balance of Payment Challenges', *Press Release*, April 13, 2022, worldbank.org/en/news/press-release/2022/04/sri-lanka-faces-unsustainable-debt-an-balance-of-payment-challenges.
14 Nichola Gordon, 'How COVID and a Nationwide Pivot to Organic Farming Pushed Sri Lanka's Economy to the Brink of Collapse', *Fortune*, April 9, 2022.
15 Sri Lanka was a British Colony till 1948. It got its independence in 1948.
16 The Korean War took place between June 1950 to July 1953.
17 Jayanti Ghosh and CP Chandrasekhar, 'The Roots of Sri Lanka's Debilitating Debt Trap', *The Hindu Business Line*, May 2, 2022.
18 Elibrary.imf.org/view/journals/002/1997/095/article-A005-en-xml.
19 The Special Drawing Rights or SDR, an interest-bearing international reserve created by the IMF that supplemented the reserve assets of member countries, is based on a basket of currencies.
20 History of Lending Commitments as of September 30, 2018, imf.org/external/np/fin/tad.
21 P Ramakumar, 'Roots of Sri Lanka's Economic Crisis', *Frontline*, April 22, 2022.
22 Current Account Deficit or CAD is the shortfall between the inflow of money on account of exports and the outflow of money on account of imports.
23 Amol Agrawal, 'How Sri Lanka Reached This Economic Precipice', April 4, 2022, moneycontrol.com/news/opinion/how-sri-lanka-reached-this-economic-precipice-8314151.html.
24 International Sovereign bonds or market borrowings from international capital markets were bonds issued by the government for borrowings in foreign currency.

25 Headquartered in Manila, the Philippines, Asian Development Bank or ADB provided loans, technical assistance, grants, and equity investments to member countries in Asia and the Pacific to promote social and economic development.
26 'Lankan PM Rajapaksa Resigns Following Weeks-Long Protest', *Mint*, May 10, 2022.
27 Deutsche Welle, 'Explained; Why Sri Lanka Defaulted on Its Foreign Debt', April 15, 2022, https://frontline.thehindu.com/despatches
28 Nithyani Anandakugan, 'The Sri Lankan Civil War and Its History, Revisited in 2020', August 31, 2020, https://hir.harvard.edu/sri-lankan-civil-war/.
29 Amol Agrawal, 'How Sri Lanka Reached This Economic Precipice', April 4, 2022, moneycontrol.com/news/opinion/how-sri-lanka-reached-this-economic-precipice-8314151.html.
30 Data.worldbank.org/indicator.
31 P Ramakumar, 'Roots of Sri Lanka's Economic Crisis', *Frontline*, April 22, 2022.
32 Soumya Bhowmick, 'Farming 'Wokness' and Sri Lanka's Downfall', www.orfonline.org/expert-speak/.
33 Uditha Jayasinghe, 'Sri Lanka Needs $5 Billion, Help from China for Essentials', www.reuters.com/world/asia-pacific/. . .- 2022–06–07/.
34 Established in 1970, Asian Clearing Union is a multilateral payments arrangement to facilitate the use of national currencies and thus serve to relax the foreign exchange constraints of member countries, viz., India, Iran, Nepal, Pakistan, Sri Lanka, Bangladesh, Myanmar, Bhutan, and Maldives.
35 Rathindra Kuruwita, 'Indian Assistance to Sri Lanka: Lifeline or Chokehold?' *The Diplomat*, May 25, 2022.
36 'Sri Lanka Jumps Close to 40% in May as Shortages Persist', business-standard.com/article/international/sri-lanka-inflation-jumps-close-to-40-in-may-as-shortages-persist-122053100933_1.html.
37 Niha Masih and Hafee Farisz, 'Sri Lanka Shuts Down, Families Struggle for Food as Crisis Deepens', *The Washington Post*, June 20, 2022.
38 'Sri Lanka Cancels School Exams over Paper Shortage', March 19, 2022, hindustantimes.com.
39 The South Asian Association for Regional Cooperation (SAARC) is an economic and political organization of eight countries in South Asia established to promote economic growth, social progress, and cultural development within the South Asian region.
40 Benjamin Parkin and Mahendra Ratnaweera, 'Sri Lanka Appeals for Food Aid as Debt Crisis Worsens', *Financial Times*, June 1, 2022.

16

BANGLADESH

The Leading Star in South Asia – Can It Sustain the Momentum?

G.V. Muralidhara

Synopsis

Bangladesh celebrated the golden jubilee year of its independence in 2021 with an impressive performance of its economy during the previous decade. The country was ranked ahead of India in the global human index as well as the gender parity index. While the country stood tall in terms of economic performance compared to its South Asian peers, it also faced several challenges in its path ahead. Though the country successfully weathered the immediate impact of the COVID-19 pandemic, it would face the economic implications of the pandemic for some more years. While experts took note of the progress made by Bangladesh, its progressive economic policies, and its ability to maintain an inclusive and open society, they cautioned that its continuation on the successful trajectory cannot be taken for granted. The country needed to carefully navigate the geopolitical challenges as well as its challenges on account of climate change. Prime Minister Sheikh Hasina had a challenging task ahead to ensure that the country continued on its growth path at the same time maintaining an inclusive and open society.

Introduction

On September 4, 2022, Sheikh Hasina (Hasina), the Prime Minister of Bangladesh allayed apprehensions that Bangladesh would face economic crisis similar to Sri Lanka[1] and said that the government of Bangladesh followed a very measured approach in taking any loans. She added that in spite of the difficulties faced due to COVID-19 pandemic and the Russia–Ukraine conflict,[2] Bangladesh's economy was in good shape.[3]

Bangladesh celebrated the golden jubilee year of its independence[4] in 2021 with an impressive performance of its economy during the previous decade. Helped by good

DOI: 10.4324/9781003261155-27

economic growth, the country reduced poverty to 9% from 19% in 2010. The country achieved impressive growth of 15% in exports, becoming a global leader in garment exports, next only to China. It also achieved significant improvement in other measures of human development, namely life expectancy (72 years) and female labour participation rate (37%) (see Figures 16.1–16.3).

The country was ranked ahead of India in the global human index as well as the gender parity index. Experts pointed out that Bangladesh's impressive performance was an apt

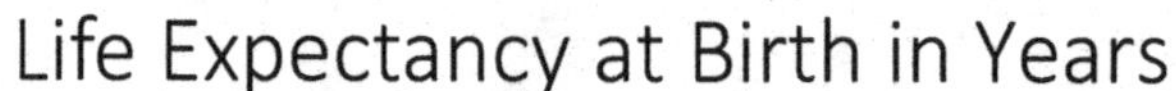

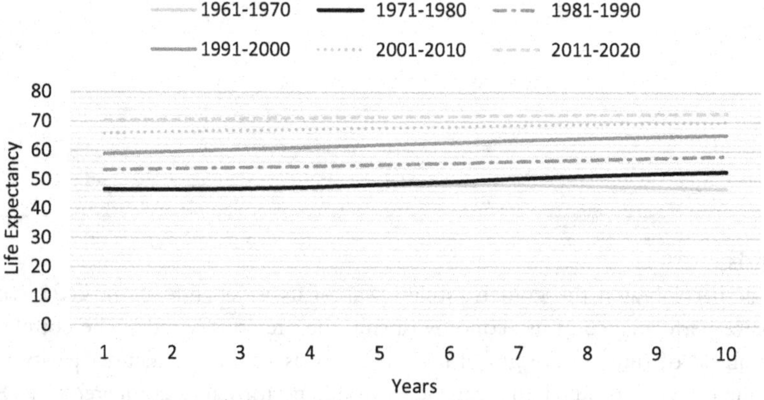

FIGURE 16.1 Life expectancy at birth.

Source: www.data.worldbank.org

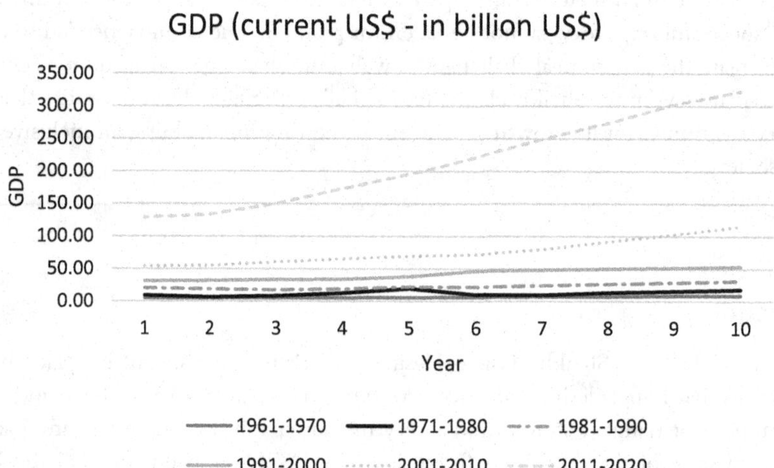

FIGURE 16.2 Bangladesh: trend of GDP (1961–2020).

Source: www.data.worldbank.org

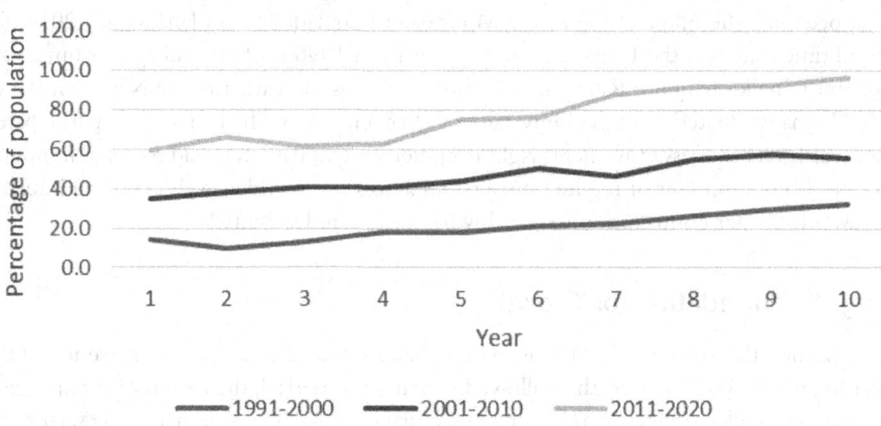

FIGURE 16.3 Access to electricity.

Source: www.data.worldbank.org

reply to the critics who had written off the country as a 'basket case' at the time of its independence.[5]

The country was also able to weather the impact of the COVID-19 pandemic successfully and maintain its growth momentum.

While the country stood tall in terms of economic performance compared to its South Asian peers, it also faced several challenges in its path ahead. While experts took note of the progress made by Bangladesh, its progressive economic policies and its ability to maintain an inclusive and open society, they cautioned that its continuation on the successful trajectory cannot be taken for granted. The country needed to carefully navigate the geopolitical challenges as well as its challenges on account of climate change.[6] It was to be seen how Prime Minister Hasina would ensure that the country continued on its growth path, at the same time maintaining an inclusive and open society.

Background

Bangladesh: Finding Its Feet

In 1947, after the end of British rule in the Indian subcontinent, when India and Pakistan became independent nations, Pakistan consisted of East and West Pakistan, separated by more than 1,500 km of Indian territory. In 1971, in a civil war led by the Awami League and assisted by India, East Pakistan proclaimed independence and became Bangladesh. Though Bangladesh went through a series of regime changes, elected governments interrupted by periods of martial law and coups between 1971 and 1996, it managed to maintain a steady growth of its economy. The country also faced frequent floods and widespread devastation. The country's per capita GDP grew steadily from $133 (current US$) in 1971 to $306 in 1990 and $394 in 1996.[7] During this period, the country also made significant progress in human development.

Sheikh Hasina

Hasina, occupied the office of the Prime Minister of Bangladesh from January 12, 2014, for the third time. She was the Prime Minister earlier from 1996 to 2001 and again from 2009. Daughter of Sheikh Mujibur Rahman, who was known as the Father of the Nation in Bangladesh, Hasina graduated from the University of Dhaka in 1973. She had actively participated as a student leader in mass movements right from her student days. She had received honorary doctorates from a number of reputed universities across the world as well as several international awards for her contribution to social work, peace, and stability.[8]

Laying the Foundation for Growth

Experts termed the years 1996–2000 as the incubation years for Bangladesh since it laid the foundation for the growth years that followed. During this period, the country made progress in developing its telecom sector and the manufacturing sector. The manufacturing sector also helped in women's empowerment as it provided employment to a large number of women.[9] The agriculture sector made significant progress during this period through the introduction of high-yielding varieties.

Bangladesh 2006–2020: A Phase of Rapid Growth

Bangladesh's GDP grew at a faster pace from 2006 onwards and helped it reach a per capita GDP of US$1962 in 2020 (see Figure 16.4). During this period, the country also made progress on other fronts. Access to electricity improved from 50.5% of the population to 96.2% of the population. Individuals using the internet improved from 1% in 2006 to 24.8% in 2020. The growth was aided by a steady flow of personal remittances from US$5.43 billion to

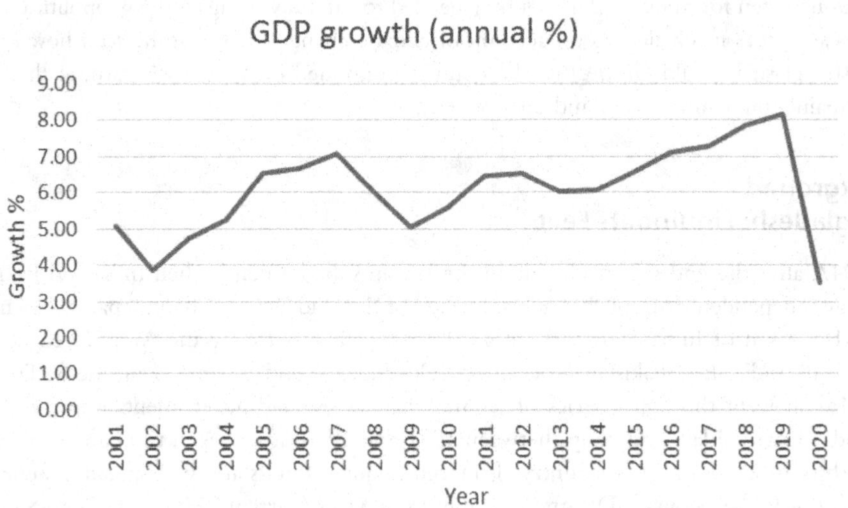

FIGURE 16.4 Bangladesh: trend of GDP growth.

Source: www.data.worldbank.org

US$21.75 billion in 2020 (see Figures 16.5 and 16.6). The country was also able to weather the COVID-19 pandemic well and maintained a growth rate of 3.5% in 2020.

The Role of NGOs

Non-governmental organizations (NGOs) played a vital role in the sustained development of Bangladesh and in making it inclusive. Experts pointed out that the government's policies and encouragement given to these organizations helped in the creation and growth of many successful NGOs in the country. Bangladesh had one of the largest non-governmental

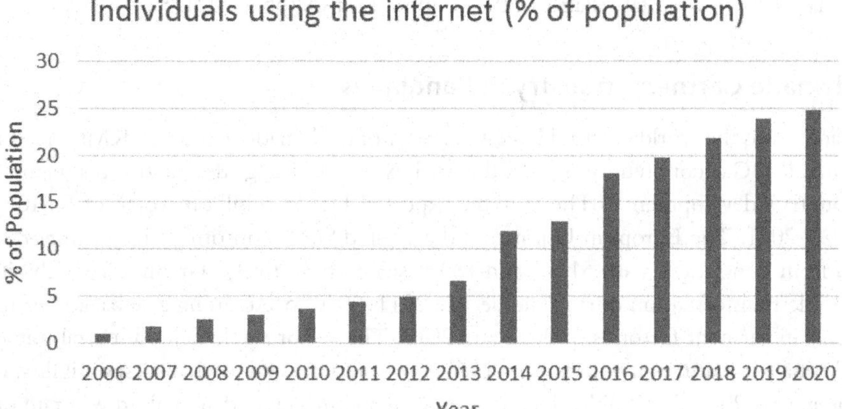

FIGURE 16.5 Access to internet.

Source: www.data.worldbank.org

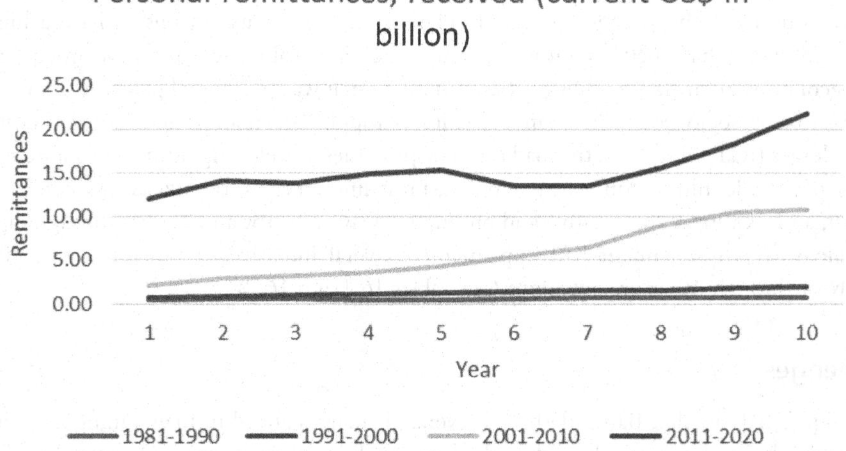

FIGURE 16.6 Bangladesh: trend of personal remittances received.

Source: www.data.worldbank.org

organization sectors in the world and had a total of 26,000 domestic NGOs as well as many more international NGOs.[10] The government had created Bangladesh NGO Foundation under the Financial Institutions Division of the Ministry of Finance to support the NGOs and to associate them with the development of the country.

Founded in 1972, BRAC, an NGO, had done pioneering work in the areas of human rights, social empowerment, education, health, and the environment. It had also set up BRAC Bank to provide banking solutions to small and medium enterprises that did not have access to traditional banking channels.[11] Grameen Bank, a non-traditional bank, had created a banking system based on mutual trust without the need for collateral from borrowers that were necessary for the conventional banking system. Grameen Bank had 9.44 million members, of which 97% were women, and was providing services in 81,768 villages covering more than 93% of the total villages in the country as of October 2021.[12]

Readymade Garment Industry in Bangladesh

Bangladesh was the world's second largest exporter of readymade garments (RMG) next only to China. RMG accounted for 81% of the total exports of Bangladesh and was a mainstay in the country's development.[13] The country exported US$31.5 billion worth of RMG during 2020–2021. The European Union and the United States constituted major importers of RMG from Bangladesh with 61.8% and 18.9% share, respectively. The industry exhibited a remarkable transformation during the decade 2011–2020, overcoming a setback after major accidents in garment factories in 2012 and 2013. The sector implemented several initiatives to make it a frontrunner in transparency on factory safety and value-chain responsibility. During the period 2011–2019, RMG exports grew at a compounded annual growth rate of 7% and increased its share of global exports from 4.7% to 6.7%.[14]

Vision 2021 and Digital Bangladesh

Bangladesh government created a vision of where the country wanted to be on the 50th anniversary of independence. The main goal of this vision was to make Bangladesh a middle-income country, with poverty eradicated. The vision was for its citizens to have a higher standard of living, have better education, achieve better social justice, and have an equitable socio-economic environment. Digital Bangladesh, which was an integral part of Vision 2021, aimed to bring socio-economic transformation through Information and Communication Technologies (ICT). The initiative had four key priorities: developing human resources ready for the new millennium, connecting citizens, providing services to citizens in a convenient manner, and creating a competitive and productive private sector and market through digital technology. The government had implemented several initiatives in this direction, either directly or through other organizations (see Tables 16.1 and 16.2).

Challenges

Experts pointed out that Bangladesh had several challenges ahead in maintaining its growth trajectory. They pointed out that while the country did well in maintaining macroeconomic stability, this had come at the cost of insufficient investments in education, healthcare, and social protection. This had impacted social development. There were also concerns about

TABLE 16.1 Digital Bangladesh: Initiatives

- Affordable access to voice and data services for e-learning in primary and secondary schools
- Promoting digital literacy
- Access to formal and informal health-related information through mobile networks and digital health services
- Dissemination of information through digital channels to improve agricultural productivity
- Access to financial services through mobile channels

Source: Bangladesh: driving mobile-enabled digital transformation, www.gsmaintelligence.com

TABLE 16.2 Projects for Expanding Digital Access

- WowBox App by Grameenphone: a lifestyle app without any data charges
- Initiatives for expanding 3G coverage in rural Bangladesh: addressing coverage and social inclusion issues
- Robi Internet4U: campaign to promote safe and proper use of internet among college and university students

Source: Bangladesh: driving mobile-enabled digital transformation, www.gsmaintelligence.com

the low tax-to-GDP ratio.[15] The country had to maintain its economic progress, maintain a good record on democracy and human rights, and not allow a turn towards authoritarianism.[16] The country also had to contend with new competition from countries like Vietnam in the global RMG market and maintain its market share. Moreover, the economy depended majorly on a single industry and this could make it vulnerable to changes in the dynamics of this industry globally.

In addition, the country had to contend with the challenges posed by climate change.

Bangladesh was situated in a low-lying river delta formed by the sedimentary deposits of the three rivers – the Ganges, the Brahmaputra, and the Meghna, which flowed from the Himalayan mountain to the Bay of Bengal. The country was predominantly low-lying and flat land. It had a network of 230 major rivers and thousands of tributaries and canals. Floods and riverbank erosions affected around 1 million people annually. Once every three to five years, up to two-thirds of the country was affected by floods. Floods affected a more significant portion of the population compared to other natural hazards. The country was also affected by cyclones. During the first two decades of the twenty-first century, 60% of the deaths caused by cyclones worldwide occurred in Bangladesh.

The country had been dealing with the challenges caused by climate change through various measures. Salt-tolerant varieties of rice were made available for farmers to cultivate. The country had also installed suitable cyclone warning and evacuation programmes and minimized the loss of lives due to these.

The country had to prepare itself for the uncertainty posed by climate change and the dangers posed by rising sea levels.

Looking Ahead

The decade following the 50th anniversary of independence was a crucial period for Bangladesh. Having drawn accolades for its impressive performance during the 50 years post-independence, the country had to balance economic development with social development as well as perform well on democracy and human rights. Analysts pointed out that Hasina had followed a system of autocracy with serious violation of human rights and oppression of freedom of speech in the country.[17] Foreign direct investment was low at 1% of the GDP. The country had to work on reducing income equality in the economy. The percentage share of the richest 10% stood at 27% of the income, and the share of the bottom 40% stood at 21%. Malnutrition needed to be addressed as 36% of children under 5 years of age suffered from malnutrition. The country had the vision to eliminate extreme poverty and secure upper middle-income country status by 2031.[18] Opinions were divided if the country will be able to continue its march on performance or will get stuck in the middle-income trap. Hasina's performance in eradicating poverty and making Bangladesh a middle-income country was being watched keenly.

Reflective Questions

1. Identify the factors that contributed to the steady growth of Bangladesh over the years making it a star performer among South Asian nations.
2. Create a roadmap for Bangladesh to continue on its growth path and address areas of concern.
3. Analyse how Bangladesh took advantage of NGOs in its development. What can developing countries learn from this?
4. What should be the immediate priorities for Sheikh Hasina?

Activities

1. Go through the data on the trend of development of the countries in South Asia and make a comparison of Bangladesh with it peers.
2. Study the impact of COVID-19 pandemic on important growth metrics of South Asian nations and compare these with other regions. Prepare a report on the resilience of the economies of South Asian nations vis-à-vis other regions.

Notes

1 In 2022, Sri Lanka faced a severe economic and forex crisis resulting in the country defaulting on external loan repayments.
2 In 2022, Russia and Ukraine were engaged in a military conflict.
3 'Sheikh Hasina Says Bangladesh Will Not Face Sri Lanka – Type Crisis, Here's Why', September 4, 2022, ndtv.com.
4 Bangladesh got its independence in 1971. It was earlier a part of Pakistan. The country was liberated from Pakistan through a civil war with the aid of Indian army.
5 Ajit Ranade, 'Why Bangladesh Has Left India Behind', https://timesofindia.indiatimes.com/india/why-bangladesh.
6 Kaushik Basu, 'The Bangladesh Economy: Navigating the Turning Point', https://direct.mit.edu/itgg/article-pdf/13/1-2/28/1978760/innov_a_00281.pdf.
7 www.data.worldbank.org.
8 'The Honourable Prime Minister', bhcanberra.com/about-bangladesh/gob/honourable-prime-minister.
9 Kaushik Basu, 'The Bangladesh Economy: Navigating the Turning Point', https://direct.mit.edu/itgg/article-pdf/13/1-2/28/1978760/innov_a_00281.pdf.
10 www.adb.org/sites/default/files/publication/28964/csb-ban-pdf.

11 www.brac.net.
12 www.grameenbank.org/introduction.
13 www.bgmea.com.bd/page/Export-Performance.
14 Achim Berg, Harsh Chhparia, Saskia Hedrich, and Karl-Hendrik Magnus, 'What's Next for Bangladesh's Garment Industry, After a Decade of Growth?' March 25, 2021, mckinsey.com/industries/retail/our-insights/whats-next-for-bangladesh-garment-industry-after-a-decade-of-growth.
15 Selim Rahman, 'Economic Challenges That Budget 2022–23 Must Address', *The Daily Star*, June 5, 2022.
16 Sali Tripathy, 'Bangladesh's Long Journey from "Basket Case" to Rising Star', https://foreignpolicy.com.
17 Noor E Julfiqar, 'Sheikh Hasina as Prime Minister of Bangladesh Is a Disaster – What Security Analysts Say', *Times of Assam*, December 28, 2018.
18 Muhammad Mahmood, 'A Critical Review of Five Decades of Bangladesh Economy', *The Financial Express*, June 26, 2021.

INDEX

Note: Page numbers in *italics* indicate a figure and page numbers in **bold** indicate a table on the corresponding page.